I CAN SAY THE R SOUND!

Speech Therapy Workbook

MEREDITH AVREN, M.ED., CCC-SLP

Hello Fabulous SLP!

We all know that teaching R can be a challenge. That's why we created this systematic, step-by-step workbook to help SLPs teach R. This workbook, **I Can Say the R Sound**, has helped hundreds of clinicians over the years. It takes you from eliciting a child's first R sound all the way through practice in oral reading and carryover to conversation.

We also created this **Sound by Sound™** card deck to make teaching that tricky R sound a little easier. The mouth pictures were drawn by Peachie Speechie's designer, Josh, to emphasize placement of articulators. Whether you are doing quick word drills or slowly focusing on motor movements for each sound, this deck is a great choice. Download these cards at **peachiespeechie.com**

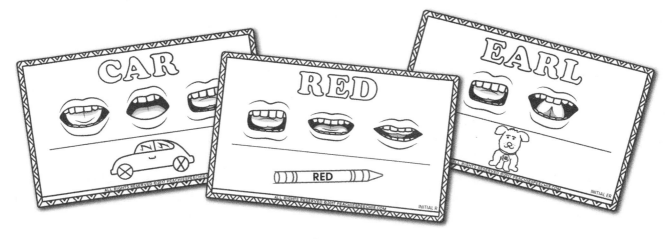

Thank you for shopping with us!
-Meredith & Josh

I CAN SAY THE R SOUND!

I Can Say the R Sound - Third Edition 2019

Library of Congress Catalog Card Number pending

ISBN 978-0-9995964-3-2
10 9 8 7 6 5 4 3 2 1

Published by Peachie Speechie®
peachiespeechie.com

TABLE OF CONTENTS

A NOTE FOR THE SPEECH-LANGUAGE PATHOLOGIST

I hope this workbook helps you as you work with your client to achieve accurate production of the R sound.

While this workbook was written for SLPs, it was also designed to be child and parent friendly. Therefore, instead of using the International Phonetic Alphabet (IPA) symbols to distinguish between /ɚ/, /ɝ/, /r/, etc., this workbook just refers to the sound as the R sound, regardless of what context is being targeted.

This workbook is a collection of instructional sheets, practice pages, and activities that have helped me successfully motivate and teach my students to produce the R sound. This workbook is not a replacement for speech therapy, of course. It is simply a collection of materials that speech-language pathologists may find useful during therapy sessions.

If you have any questions, suggestions, or comments please feel free to email me at meredith@peachiespeechie.com

Meredith Avren, M. Ed., CCC-SLP

Thank you for being a Peachie Speechie customer! You're sure to love our other **"I Can"** workbooks, including:

- I Can Say the S Sound
- I Can Say S-Blends
- I Can Say the L Sound
- I Can Say the SH Sound
- I Can Say the TH Sound
- I Can Say the K and G Sounds
- I Can Say the F and V Sounds
- I Can Say Final Consonants

- I Can Answer WH Questions
- I Can Make Inferences
- I Can Describe & Categorize
- I Can Determine the Main Idea
- I Can Have Conversations
- I Can Use Context Clues
- I Can Use Figurative Language
- I Can Use Verbs
...and more!

Just go to peachiespeechie.com and click materials!

Important disclaimer about this resource, "I Can Say the R Sound": This workbook and the techniques presented in it are designed to be used by a speech-language pathologist with an in-depth knowledge of anatomy and speech sound production. Users must use professional judgment and common sense when implementing techniques described in this product. Appropriate techniques vary based on the individual being treated.

WHY IS THE R SOUND TRICKY?

You are not alone! Many children have difficulty saying the R sound. This sound is tricky for a few reasons.

First, the R sound is kind of "hidden" in your mouth. For some sounds, you can easily see how they are made. For example, when someone says the /l/ sound, you can see their tongue tip rising up behind their front teeth. But when someone says the R sound, it can be difficult to see what exactly they are doing with their tongue.

Another reason the R sound is so tricky is because there are multiple ways to produce the same sound. Some people bunch their tongue up in the back and others curl the tip of their tongue back. Other people use both of these methods.

Additionally, the sounds around the R sound in a word can change the way your mouth and tongue move as you produce the R. For example, say the words "orange" and "red." When you say the word "orange," your jaw drops down before you get to the R, your lips round more, and it sounds a little different than the R in the word "red," doesn't it?

Even though the R sound can be challenging to learn, you can do it!

THE R SOUND IN DIFFERENT CONTEXTS

Production of the R sound is impacted by the sounds around it. Therefore, many clinicians choose to teach vocalic R as separate sounds: ER, AR, AIR, EAR, IRE , and OR. Prevocalic R and R-blends are also frequently targeted separately. Examples are listed below.

ER
Example words:
· Earnings
· Person
· Fur

AR
Example words:
· Art
· Party
· Car

AIR
Example words:
· Airplane
· Parent
· Bear

EAR
Example words:
· Earring
· Serious
· Fear

IRE
Example words:
· Ireland
· Pirate
· Wire

OR
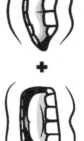
Example words:
· Orange
· Fortune
· Core

R-Blends
Blends occur when two consonants are next to each other in a word.

Example words:
· Bread
· Cry
· Tricky

Initial Prevocalic R
The R sound is the first sound in a word, followed by a vowel sound.

Example words:
· Red
· Rocket
· Ring

SELF REPORT

How is My Speech?

Do you have difficulty producing one or more speech sounds?   (YES)   (NO)   (I DON'T KNOW)

How do you feel about your speech?

Do you want to work on improving your speech?   (✓ YES)   (✗ NO)

Do you feel confident when talking to your peers?   (YES, ALWAYS)   (NO, NEVER)   (SOMETIMES)

Do other people point out differences in your speech?   (YES, ALWAYS)   (NO, NEVER)   (SOMETIMES)

Do you feel frustrated when speaking?   (YES, OFTEN)   (NO, NEVER)   (SOMETIMES)

What else would you like to tell me about your speech?

I CAN SAY THE R SOUND!

Speech Anatomy: Let's learn about parts of the mouth!

Before we start working on specific speech sounds, let's learn about the body parts used in speech production. We will learn about the following structures: lips, tongue (tip and back of the tongue), alveolar ridge, teeth (front teeth and molars), palate and jaw.

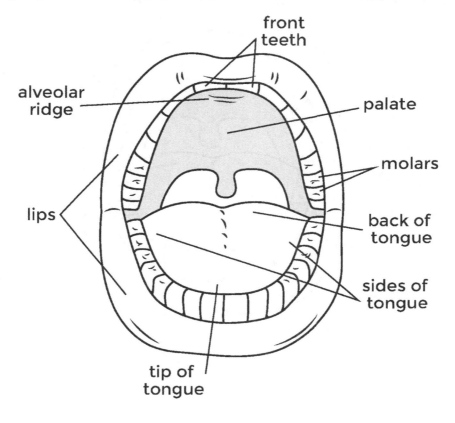

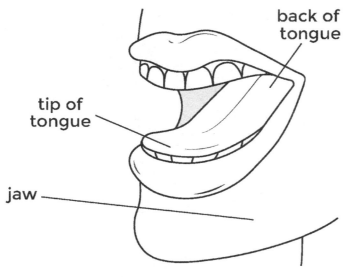

I CAN SAY THE R SOUND!

Speech Anatomy: Label the body parts below.

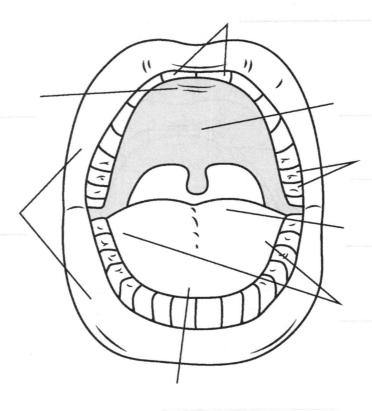

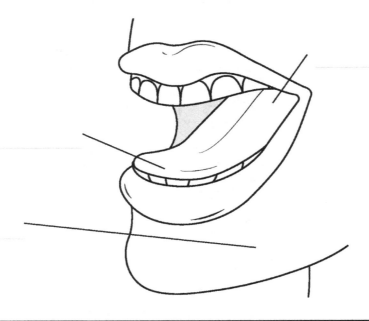

I CAN SAY THE R SOUND!

Bunched R vs. Retroflexed R: Let's learn about two ways to produce the R sound!

When people produce "Bunched R", they pull their tongue back in their mouth. The back sides of their tongue go up and touch their back molars. The tongue is tense and looks bunched up in the back of the mouth!

Bunched R

When people produce "Retroflexed R", the tip of the tongue curls up and backwards.

Retroflexed R

I CAN SAY THE R SOUND!

How to Produce the Bunched R

Slide your tongue back in your mouth.

Form a "hump" or "bunched" shape with your tongue. The back sides of your tongue will be up, touching the back molars.

Keep your tongue up and keep it tense! Turn your voice on to say the R sound. If your tongue drops down, you'll end up saying the "uhhh" sound instead.

I CAN SAY THE R SOUND!

How to Produce the Retroflexed R

Curl the tip of your tongue backwards into your mouth.

The sides of your tongue will curl up and back also.

Keeping your tongue in position, slightly close your jaw. Turn your voice on to say the R sound.

Bunched R

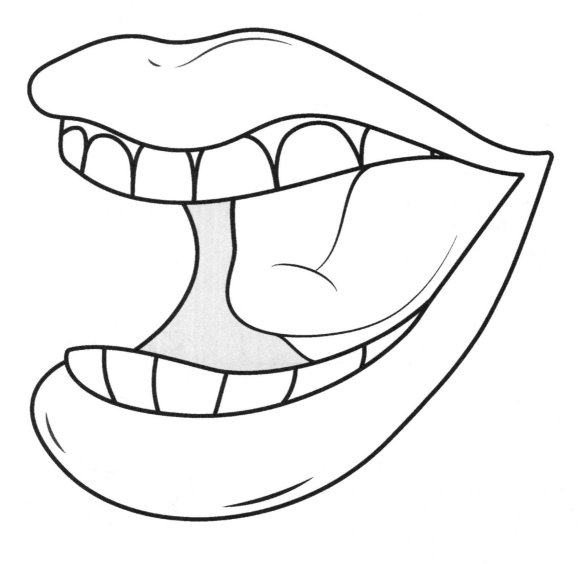

Retroflex R

I CAN SAY THE R SOUND!

How do I say the R sound?

Directions: The mouth in this picture needs a tongue! Draw what the tongue should look like when you say your R sound. Then, explain what you need to do to make your tongue look like that.

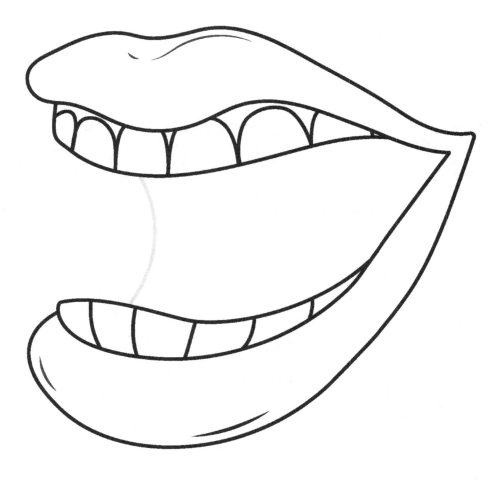

_____

_____

_____

I CAN SAY THE R SOUND!

Bunched R: Make your own tongue!

Using modeling dough, make a tongue and mold it into the shape required for production of the R sound.

1. Roll play dough into a ball.

2. Squish it into a tongue shape.

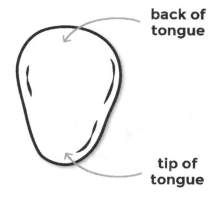

back of tongue

tip of tongue

3. Find the back sides. Bring them up to your back molars.

4. Keep the sides up and pull your whole tongue back.

I CAN SAY THE R SOUND!

Retroflexed R: Make your own tongue!

Using modeling dough, make a tongue and mold it into the shape required for production of the R sound.

1. Roll play dough into a ball.

2. Squish it into a tongue shape.

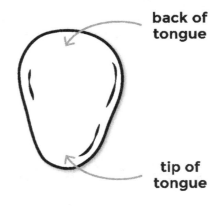

back of tongue

tip of tongue

3. Curl the tip up. The sides will curl upward as well and touch the back molars when you say the R sound.

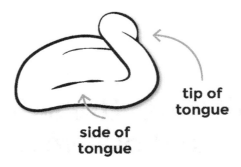

tip of tongue

side of tongue

MAKE YOUR OWN MOUTH MODEL

Cut out the paper mouth along the dotted lines. Fold along the solid gray lines. Use crayons to draw a tongue in the mouth, or laminate the mouth and use play dough to make a tongue. You can use this as a visual for tongue placement while practicing the R sound.

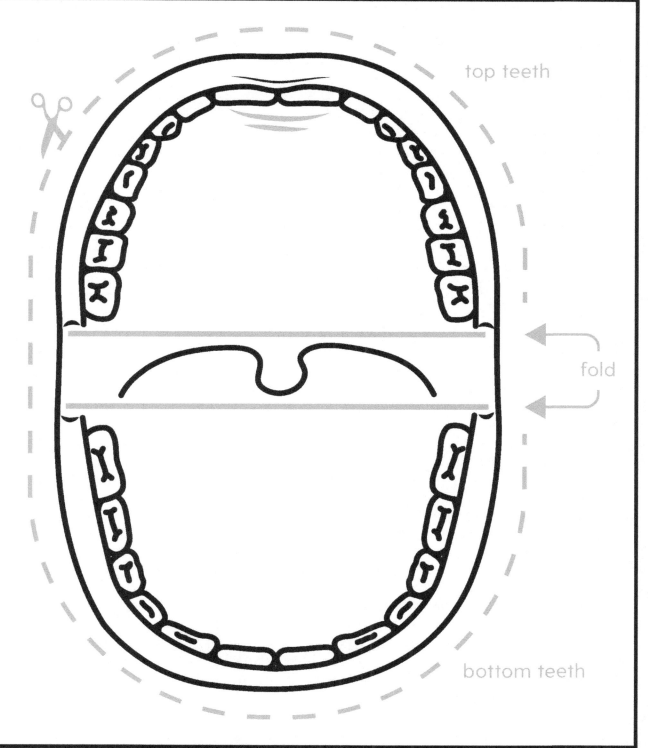

top teeth

fold

bottom teeth

I CAN SAY THE R SOUND!

Shaping an L into an R

You will start by saying the L sound. Lift your tongue tip up to your alveolar ridge. Say the L sound!

Then, slide your tongue tip a little further back along the roof of your mouth, behind the alveolar ridge and make a sound. That doesn't really sound like a normal speech sound, does it? That's OK! Keep going!

Slide your tongue tip back even more. As you slide it, keep your voice on and listen as the sound changes.

Then, close your jaw slightly.

SLIDING FROM L TO R

Slide your tongue along your palate as you go from the L sound to the R sound (retroflex position). Each time you do this, mark one of the circles below.

I CAN SAY THE R SOUND!

Holler the R Sound! Shaping Final Vocalic R

Transfer your R sound from isolation to words using this method!

1.

L ➡ R Slide

First, shape the R sound from an L sound by sliding the tip of your tongue from the alveolar ridge all the way back until it is curled into position for retroflex R. Practice the L➡R slide multiple times.

2.

Air + L ➡ R Slide

Next, position your tongue on your alveolar ridge to do the L➡R slide, but release a little bit of air before you say the L sound. You'll release a bit of air and then immediately continue your L➡R slide.

3.

Holler

Now, you are ready to HOLLER! You're going to say HA right before doing the L➡R slide. This will end up sounding like the word holler!

4.

Other L ➡ R Words

Once you have successfully said, "**holler**" several times, you can try other L➡R words such as collar, taller, and dollar.

I CAN SAY THE R SOUND!

Say each word below. Slide your tongue from the L sound into the R sound.

Scholar		He is a scholar.
Taller		Jeff is taller than Meg.
Collar		Fluffy wears a collar.
Mailer		I sent out the mailer.
Sailor		He is a sailor.
Smaller		That bee is smaller.

I CAN SAY THE R SOUND!

Say each word below. Slide your tongue from the L sound into the R sound.

Peeler		Use a peeler to peel an apple.
Color		I color with crayons.
Dollar	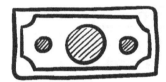	I have one dollar.
Killer		Killer is a mean dog.
Trailer		The truck pulled the trailer.
Filler		Add filler to the cracks.

I CAN SAY THE R SOUND!

Learning the R Sound

L → R Slide

Use the L→R slide (discussed on page 25) to help you say the word learning!

L   R

L → R Slide + NING

After you do the L→R slide, add NING to the end.

L   R   + **NING** = **LEARNING**

Once you can say the word **learning**, practice the phrases below:

Learning to swim ☐ ☐ ☐   Learning to sing ☐ ☐ ☐

Learning to dance ☐ ☐ ☐   Learning to knit ☐ ☐ ☐

Learning to cook ☐ ☐ ☐   Learning to paint ☐ ☐ ☐

I CAN SAY THE R SOUND!

Shaping an EE into an R

Say the EE sound. Hold it out as you think about your tongue position. You will feel the back sides of your tongue touching your back teeth.

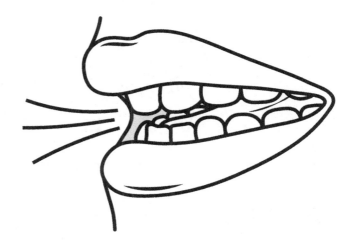

As you are saying the EE sound, pull your tongue back. Your whole tongue will slide back. You will feel the back sides of your tongue sliding back along your teeth. Listen to the sound change. It will sound like you said the word **EAR**.

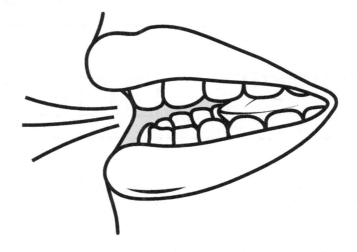

I CAN SAY THE R SOUND!

As you are saying the EE sound, pull your tongue back. Your whole tongue will slide back. You will feel the back sides of your tongue sliding back along your teeth. Listen to the sound change. It will sound like you said the word EAR. Practice doing this as you say the phrases below.

EE → **R**

Bunny ear ☐☐☐☐☐ / ☐☐☐☐☐

Puppy ear ☐☐☐☐☐ / ☐☐☐☐☐

Pony ear ☐☐☐☐☐ / ☐☐☐☐☐

Kitty ear ☐☐☐☐☐ / ☐☐☐☐☐

Monkey ear ☐☐☐☐ / ☐☐☐☐

I CAN SAY THE R SOUND!

Shaping SH into R: the SURE way to achieve accurate production!

Say the SH Sound.

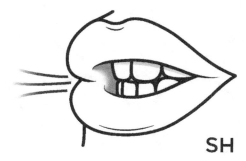

SH

As you are saying the SH sound, pull your tongue back and turn your voice on. Listen as your sound changes from SH to R.

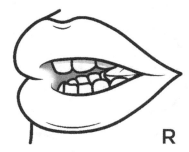

R

Do it again, a little bit quicker. You will say the word SURE!

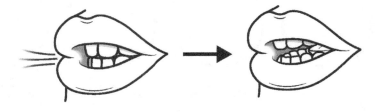

SURE

SLIDING FROM SH TO R

Slide your tongue back to go from the SH sound to the R sound (bunched position).
Each time you do this, mark one of the circles below.

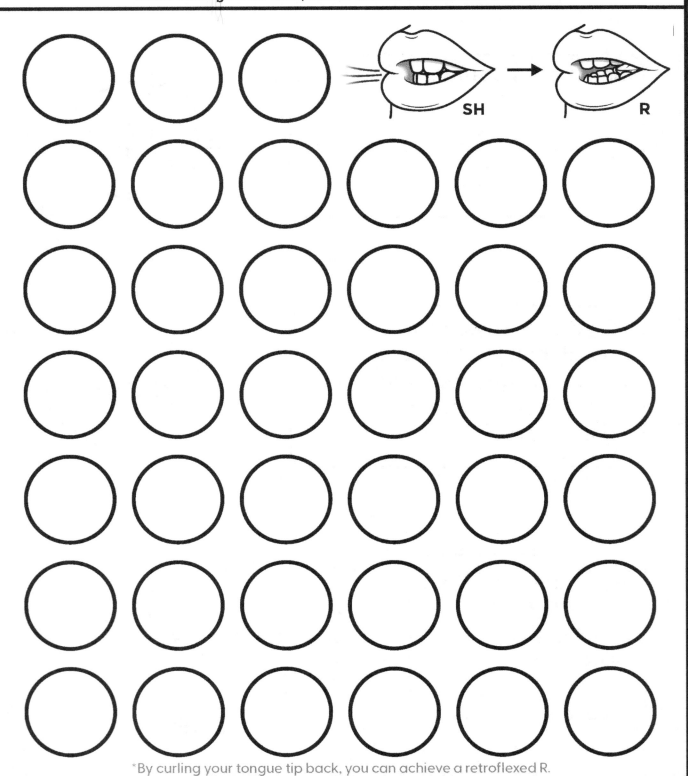

*By curling your tongue tip back, you can achieve a retroflexed R.

I CAN SAY THE R SOUND!

Start by saying the SH sound. Then, pull your tongue back to go from the SH sound to the R sound. Once you are able to do this, practice the words below. Check a box each time you practice.

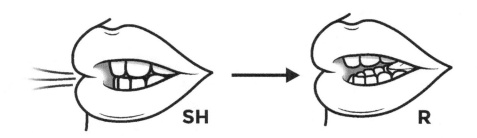

Shred ☐ ☐ ☐ ☐ ☐ ☐ ☐ ☐ ☐ ☐

Shrimp ☐ ☐ ☐ ☐ ☐ ☐ ☐ ☐ ☐ ☐

Shriek ☐ ☐ ☐ ☐ ☐ ☐ ☐ ☐ ☐ ☐

Shrub ☐ ☐ ☐ ☐ ☐ ☐ ☐ ☐ ☐ ☐

Shrink ☐ ☐ ☐ ☐ ☐ ☐ ☐ ☐ ☐ ☐

Shrill ☐ ☐ ☐ ☐ ☐ ☐ ☐ ☐ ☐ ☐

Shrug ☐ ☐ ☐ ☐ ☐ ☐ ☐ ☐ ☐ ☐

Shrek ☐ ☐ ☐ ☐ ☐ ☐ ☐ ☐ ☐ ☐

I CAN SAY THE R SOUND!

Shaping /ʒ/ into the Final R Sound

Say the /ʒ/ sound. Remember, this sound is like the SH sound with your voice turned on.

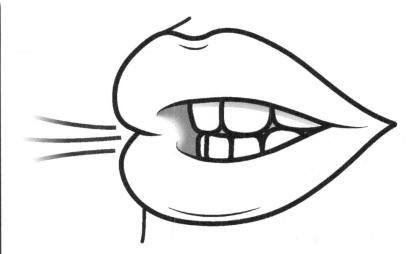

While you are saying the /ʒ/ sound, pull your tongue back. Listen as your sound changes into the R sound.

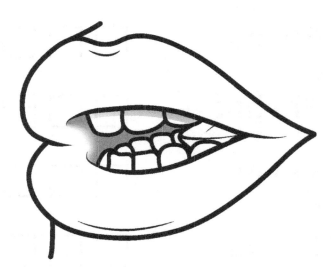

*By curling your tongue tip back, you can achieve a retroflexed R.

I CAN SAY THE R SOUND!

Start by saying the /ʒ/ sound. Then, pull your tongue back to slide into an R sound. Once you are able to do this, practice the words below. Check a box each time you practice.

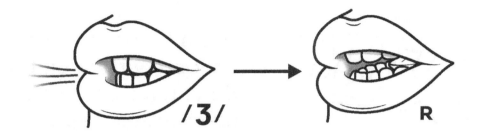

/ʒ/ → R

Measure ☐ ☐ ☐ ☐ ☐ ☐ ☐ ☐ ☐ ☐

Leisure ☐ ☐ ☐ ☐ ☐ ☐ ☐ ☐ ☐ ☐

Closure ☐ ☐ ☐ ☐ ☐ ☐ ☐ ☐ ☐ ☐

Seizure ☐ ☐ ☐ ☐ ☐ ☐ ☐ ☐ ☐ ☐

Treasure ☐ ☐ ☐ ☐ ☐ ☐ ☐ ☐ ☐ ☐

Pleasure ☐ ☐ ☐ ☐ ☐ ☐ ☐ ☐ ☐ ☐

Composure ☐ ☐ ☐ ☐ ☐ ☐ ☐ ☐ ☐ ☐

Exposure ☐ ☐ ☐ ☐ ☐ ☐ ☐ ☐ ☐ ☐

*By curling your tongue tip back, you can achieve a retroflexed R.

BALLOON VISUAL

Sometimes, a client may have their tongue positioned correctly, but lack adequate tension to achieve a clear and accurate R sound. I came up with this balloon visual to help teach placement for bunched R while also emphasizing muscle tension.

Use a funnel to fill a balloon with flour. If you don't have a funnel, a plastic disposable water bottle can be cut in half to create one. A straw can be used to help press the flour into the balloon.

Tie off the end of the balloon and brush clean any excess flour.

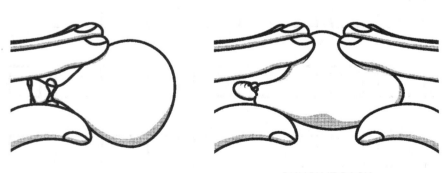

BUNCH IT BACK

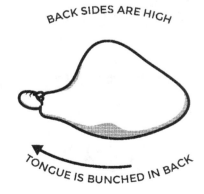

BACK SIDES ARE HIGH

TONGUE IS BUNCHED IN BACK

BALLOON VISUAL

It's time to focus on TENSION! Your tongue needs to be in the correct position for R, which includes making it tense when you say the sound. You will be tightening your tongue. A flour-filled balloon can be a useful visual for tongue tension.

BALLOON TONGUE

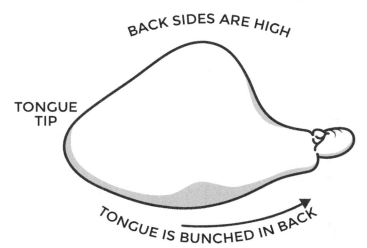

BACK SIDES ARE HIGH

TONGUE TIP

TONGUE IS BUNCHED IN BACK

First, shape your balloon into the bunched R shape as shown on page 36.

Squeeze the balloon in your palm to show tension. Practice saying your R sound as you squeeze.

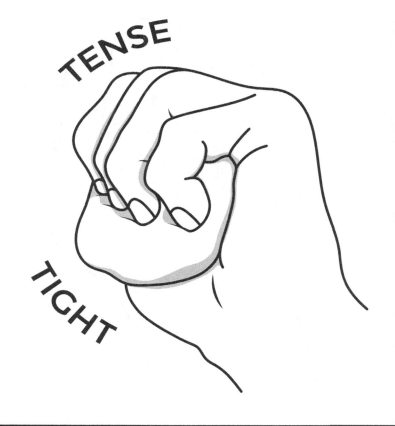

TENSE

TIGHT

FEEL THE TENSION

Your tongue will need to be tense to acheive an accurate R sound. Gently feel your clinician's throat as they say, "uhhh" and then say, "RRR". Did you feel the change? Place your thumb on your own throat and feel the tension as you say the R sound. You (or your SLP) can also gently press up on this spot to encourage a high, tense tongue.

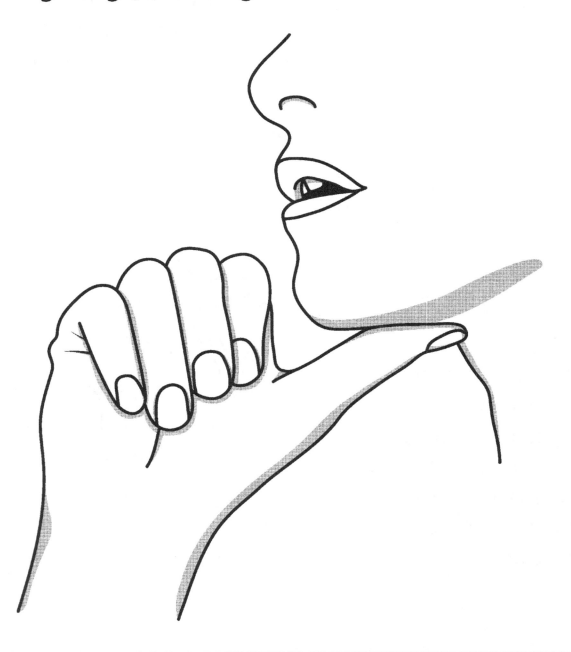

I CAN SAY THE R SOUND!

Tools for Teaching the R Sound

Sometimes verbal placement instructions, models, and illustrations are not enough to teach a child to say the R sound. For these children, additional tactile input can be helpful. The following tools can be used to increase a child's awareness of their oral structures and help guide their tongue into the correct position. Each child is different, and it is up to their speech-language pathologist to decide which tools are most appropriate during therapy sessions.

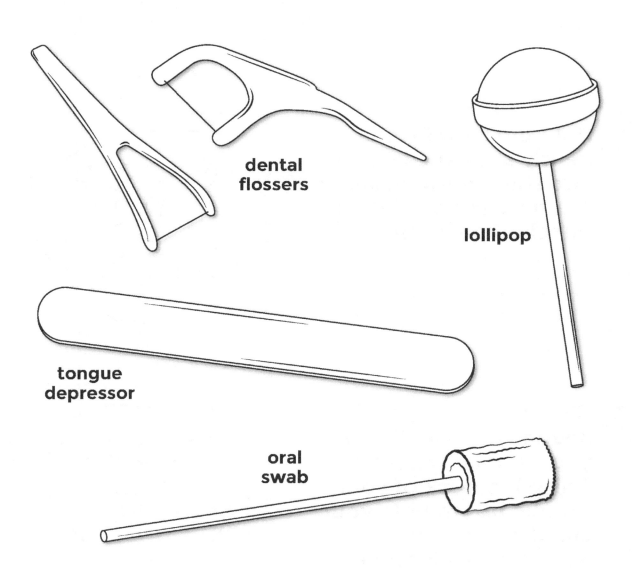

dental flossers

lollipop

tongue depressor

oral swab

I CAN SAY THE R SOUND!

Dental Flossers for Bunched R

1. Position the flosser with the floss-side facing up.

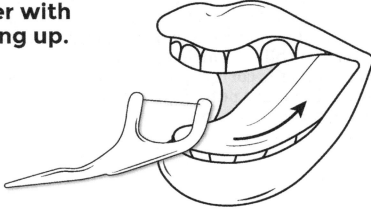

2. Hold the handle and gently slide the flosser into the mouth, pushing the tongue back into a bunched position.

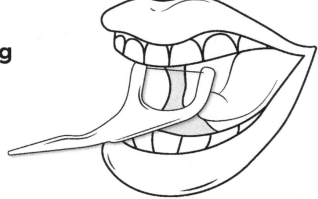

3. Give verbal prompts as needed such as "keep your tongue tense" or "raise the back of your tongue up" to help your client achieve an accurate production.

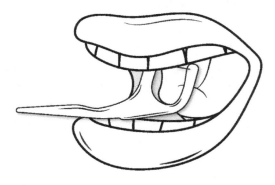

I CAN SAY THE R SOUND!

Dental Flossers for Retroflexed R

1. Hold the flosser handle, with the floss-side facing the client's mouth.

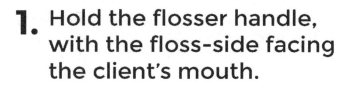

2. Ask them to curl their tongue around the floss and pull it back into their mouth.

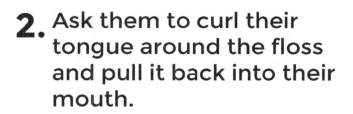

3. Have them close their jaw a little bit around the flosser, keeping the tongue in a curled, retroflexed position.

I CAN SAY THE R SOUND!

Lollipops, Tongue Depressors, and Oral Swabs

Since R is such a difficult sound to see in the mouth, some children may benefit from tactile stimulation in addition to models and verbal placement instruction. Touching the back lateral margins of the tongue and the inner gums just above the back molars may help increase awareness of the articulators and tongue placement required for the R sound. The following instructions encourage the production of a bunched R.

1. Introduce your client to the item you will be using for this exercise (lollipop, tongue depressor, or oral swab). The client might want to touch the item before you put it in their mouth. Be sure they wash their hands first.

2. Using a therapy mirror, instruct your client to stick out their tongue.

3. When the client sticks out their tongue, rub the back lateral margins of the tongue with a tongue depressor, lollipop, or oral swab.

4. Next, rub the inner gums just above the back teeth.

5. Instruct your client to touch the back sides of their tongue to the inner gums above the molars.

6. Instruct your client to hold their tongue in that position while they turn their voice on to produce the R sound.

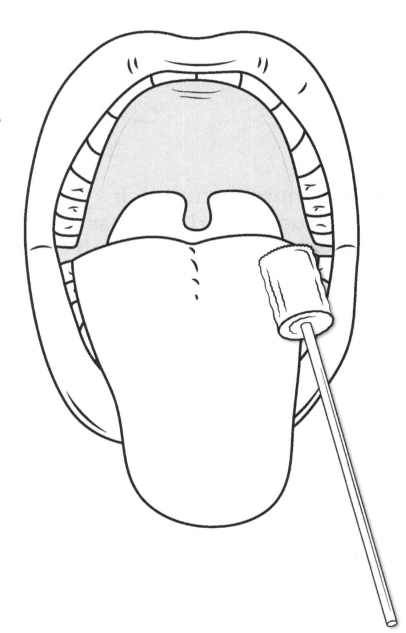

I CAN SAY THE R SOUND!

Stabilizing the Jaw for Production of R

If your client is sliding their jaw or drops their jaw too much when attempting to produce the R sound, a bite block may be helpful in stabilizing their jaw. You can purchase a bite block from a dental supply store, or you can use a skinny tongue depressor (popsicle stick), coffee straw, or the handle of an oral swab as a bite block. Place the bite block/item in the client's mouth between the back molars on one side. Make sure to emphasize to your client that the R sound is mainly formed by moving the tongue. The jaw and lips remain still during production of the R sound.

When you're first teaching the client to isolate tongue movement from jaw movement, it may help to use the tongue depressor/popsicle stick vertically, along the thin edge as shown in the illustration to prop the mouth open enough for the client to be able to see their tongue movement in a mirror. A pen light may also be helpful here.

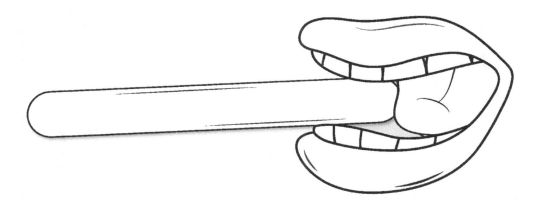

Once the client understands the appropriate tongue placement, moving to a thinner object such as a coffee straw or the handle of an oral swab can be used instead. For accurate acoustic quality in production of R, having the jaw closed more instead of being propped wide open is best.

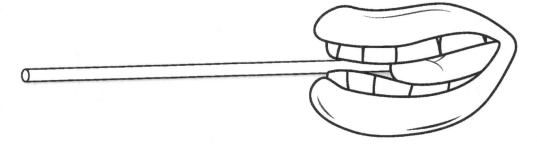

HAND CUES: VISUALS FOR TONGUE POSITION

One of the simplest ways to demonstrate tongue movement for the R sound is with hand cues. Different hand cues can be used to show the bunched vs. retroflexed positions. Using hand cues is common in multisensory approaches for speech sound disorders and has shown to assist in remediation of the R sound when used in combination with verbal instructions in a single subject study (Rusiewicz & Rivera, 2017).

Start by flattening your hand to illustrate what your tongue looks like at rest. Then, move it into the bunched or retroflexed positions as shown below.

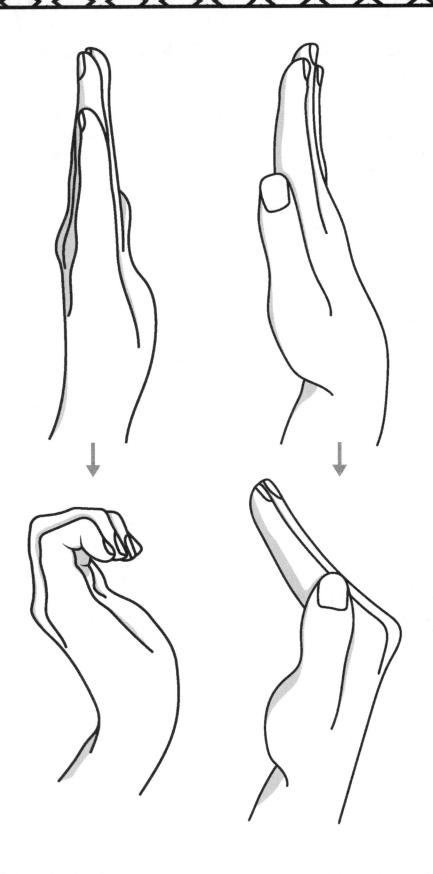

I CAN SAY THE R SOUND!

R Sound Visuals

GRRRRRR

ARRRRRR

ERRR ERRR ERRR

RRRRRRR

REDUCE LIP ROUNDING WITH THE EE SOUND

Substituting the W sound for the R sound is a common error. When the W sound is produced, our lips are rounded. Therefore, selecting target words that encourage lip retraction can be helpful in achieving accurate productions of initial R. Use a mirror to complete the activity below.

EE

Say EEEE as you look in the mirror. Notice how your lips are pulled back. You can even smile while you say EEE.

W

Now say the W sound. Notice how your lips look different. They are rounded.

Let's practice R words that have the EE sound in them to help keep your lips retracted and avoid the W sound. Check a box each time you practice.

R → **EE**

READ	☐ ☐ ☐	REFLECT	☐ ☐ ☐
REASON	☐ ☐ ☐	RELATE	☐ ☐ ☐
REMIX	☐ ☐ ☐	REPEAT	☐ ☐ ☐
RECYCLE	☐ ☐ ☐	RETURN	☐ ☐ ☐
REMIND	☐ ☐ ☐	REHEAT	☐ ☐ ☐

LIP ROUNDING AND COARTICULATION

The sounds that come before and after the R in a word can influence the way your mouth moves and how you say R. This is called coarticulation. This is important to consider when selecting target words for therapy. If a child is substituting W for the R sound, you may be more successful selecting target words that encourage lip retraction such as "re-" words instead of words that encourage lip rounding such as "roo" words.

Say the words below. Notice how your lips are positioned when you say the R sound.

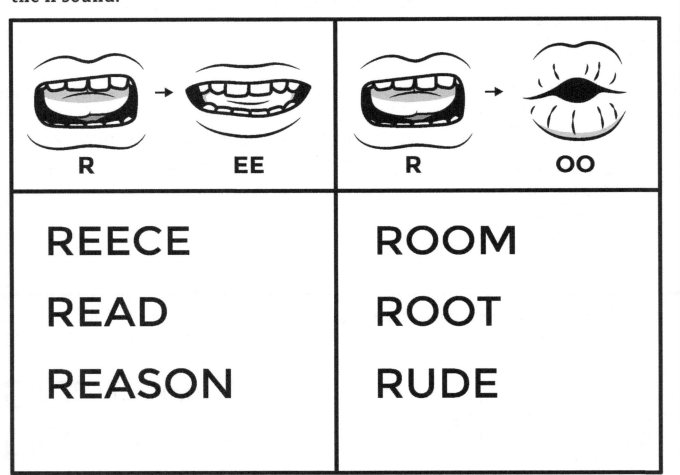

R → EE	R → OO
REECE	ROOM
READ	ROOT
REASON	RUDE

Clinicians may choose to start therapy with "re-" words and once the child has mastered them, select more difficult targets such as "roo" words.

SAYING KR AND GR WORDS

Since production of the K and G sounds require the tongue to be elevated in the back, it can be helpful to use KR and GR blends when practicing the R sound. Try practicing the words below!

GROW

GRAPEFRUIT

CRANE

CRY

CROW

GROWL

CRAB

CRACKED

GRADUATE

GRILL

GREEN

GRAPES

I CAN SAY THE R SOUND!

Since production of the G sound requires your tongue to be elevated in the back, practicing GR blends can help you achieve accurate production of bunched R. Practice the GR words below and mark a box for every production. If you fill all the boxes, you will have practiced 100 times!

Grow ☐ ☐ ☐ ☐ ☐ ☐ ☐ ☐ ☐ ☐

Great ☐ ☐ ☐ ☐ ☐ ☐ ☐ ☐ ☐ ☐

Gross ☐ ☐ ☐ ☐ ☐ ☐ ☐ ☐ ☐ ☐

Graph ☐ ☐ ☐ ☐ ☐ ☐ ☐ ☐ ☐ ☐

Grade ☐ ☐ ☐ ☐ ☐ ☐ ☐ ☐ ☐ ☐

Green ☐ ☐ ☐ ☐ ☐ ☐ ☐ ☐ ☐ ☐

Groom ☐ ☐ ☐ ☐ ☐ ☐ ☐ ☐ ☐ ☐

Greedy ☐ ☐ ☐ ☐ ☐ ☐ ☐ ☐ ☐ ☐

Grandma ☐ ☐ ☐ ☐ ☐ ☐ ☐ ☐ ☐ ☐

Grumpy ☐ ☐ ☐ ☐ ☐ ☐ ☐ ☐ ☐ ☐

I CAN SAY THE R SOUND!

Since production of the G sound requires your tongue to be elevated in the back, practicing GR blends can help you achieve accurate production of bunched R. Practice the GR words below and mark a box for every production. If you fill all the boxes, you will have practiced 100 times!

G → R

Grey	☐ ☐ ☐ ☐ ☐ ☐ ☐ ☐ ☐ ☐
Grew	☐ ☐ ☐ ☐ ☐ ☐ ☐ ☐ ☐ ☐
Grip	☐ ☐ ☐ ☐ ☐ ☐ ☐ ☐ ☐ ☐
Grin	☐ ☐ ☐ ☐ ☐ ☐ ☐ ☐ ☐ ☐
Grab	☐ ☐ ☐ ☐ ☐ ☐ ☐ ☐ ☐ ☐
Grits	☐ ☐ ☐ ☐ ☐ ☐ ☐ ☐ ☐ ☐
Greek	☐ ☐ ☐ ☐ ☐ ☐ ☐ ☐ ☐ ☐
Great	☐ ☐ ☐ ☐ ☐ ☐ ☐ ☐ ☐ ☐
Group	☐ ☐ ☐ ☐ ☐ ☐ ☐ ☐ ☐ ☐
Gravy	☐ ☐ ☐ ☐ ☐ ☐ ☐ ☐ ☐ ☐

I CAN SAY THE R SOUND!

Since production of the K sound requires your tongue to be elevated in the back, practicing KR blends can help you achieve accurate production of bunched R. Practice the KR words below and mark a box for every production. If you fill all the boxes, you will have practiced 100 times!

K → R

Crow ☐ ☐ ☐ ☐ ☐ ☐ ☐ ☐ ☐ ☐

Cry ☐ ☐ ☐ ☐ ☐ ☐ ☐ ☐ ☐ ☐

Crew ☐ ☐ ☐ ☐ ☐ ☐ ☐ ☐ ☐ ☐

Crab ☐ ☐ ☐ ☐ ☐ ☐ ☐ ☐ ☐ ☐

Crib ☐ ☐ ☐ ☐ ☐ ☐ ☐ ☐ ☐ ☐

Crime ☐ ☐ ☐ ☐ ☐ ☐ ☐ ☐ ☐ ☐

Crate ☐ ☐ ☐ ☐ ☐ ☐ ☐ ☐ ☐ ☐

Crush ☐ ☐ ☐ ☐ ☐ ☐ ☐ ☐ ☐ ☐

Croak ☐ ☐ ☐ ☐ ☐ ☐ ☐ ☐ ☐ ☐

Crown ☐ ☐ ☐ ☐ ☐ ☐ ☐ ☐ ☐ ☐

I CAN SAY THE R SOUND!

Since production of the K sound requires your tongue to be elevated in the back, practicing KR blends can help you achieve accurate production of bunched R. Practice the KR words below and mark a box for every production. If you fill all the boxes, you will have practiced 100 times!

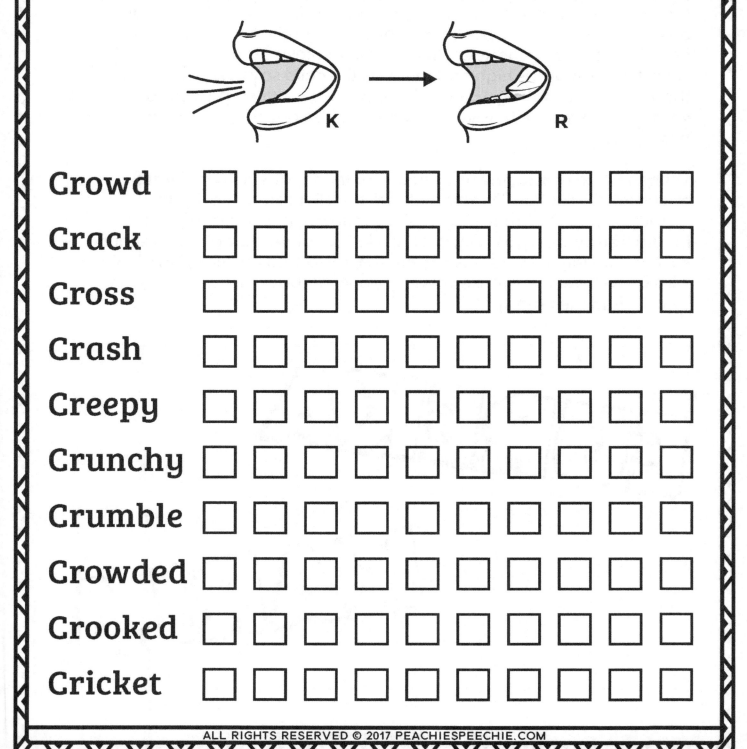

Crowd ☐ ☐ ☐ ☐ ☐ ☐ ☐ ☐ ☐ ☐

Crack ☐ ☐ ☐ ☐ ☐ ☐ ☐ ☐ ☐ ☐

Cross ☐ ☐ ☐ ☐ ☐ ☐ ☐ ☐ ☐ ☐

Crash ☐ ☐ ☐ ☐ ☐ ☐ ☐ ☐ ☐ ☐

Creepy ☐ ☐ ☐ ☐ ☐ ☐ ☐ ☐ ☐ ☐

Crunchy ☐ ☐ ☐ ☐ ☐ ☐ ☐ ☐ ☐ ☐

Crumble ☐ ☐ ☐ ☐ ☐ ☐ ☐ ☐ ☐ ☐

Crowded ☐ ☐ ☐ ☐ ☐ ☐ ☐ ☐ ☐ ☐

Crooked ☐ ☐ ☐ ☐ ☐ ☐ ☐ ☐ ☐ ☐

Cricket ☐ ☐ ☐ ☐ ☐ ☐ ☐ ☐ ☐ ☐

EUREKA AND KARLA: HELPFUL WORDS

There are several words that have been popular among speech-language pathologists for teaching the R sound. One is **Eureka** (Henderson Jones, 2004) and another is **Karla**. These two words are thought to be helpful for teaching the R sound because the sounds around the R sound help it get into position. Eureka and Karla take coarticulation into consideration to help achieve production of the R sound. The tongue is high and tense as the child says the Y sound and then moves into saying, "Eureka." Henderson suggests phrases beginning with the Y sound such as **you're ready**, **you're reading**, etc. when practicing.

With the word **Karla**, the movements of the tongue help facilitate accurate production. For this method, the client says, "ka-la, ka-la," and as they say the "la," they slide their tongue back along the roof of the mouth (retroflexed position) until "ka-la" becomes "Karla". I have found success having my students say **car key** (bunched position), **earring**, and **Kira** as well because tense vowels and velar (back) sounds, help the tongue find the right spot.

KARLA

The word Karla is often used to elicit vocalic R using the retroflexed tongue position. Follow the steps below to try this method.

Say Ka-La

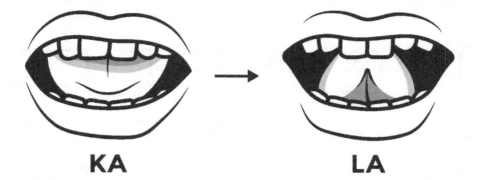

KA → **LA**

Say Ka-La repeatedly, moving your tongue tip back along your palate a little more with each production.

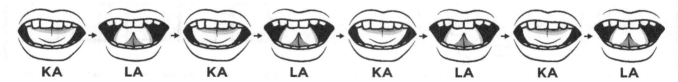

KA → LA → KA → LA → KA → LA → KA → LA

As the top of your tongue moves backwards, the L sound will gradually become an R sound, turning Ka-La into Karla! Once you start to hear a good R sound, be sure to flick your tongue tip forward to also produce a clear L sound after the R.

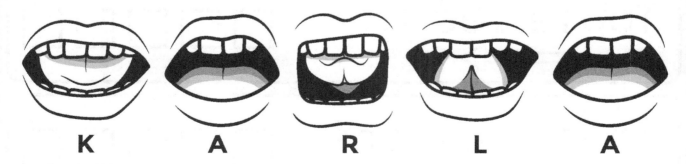

K   A   R   L   A

I CAN SAY THE R SOUND!

You're ready to practice the R sound!

Sliding into an initial R from a final vocalic R can help you say it correctly. Say the first word and connect it to the second word. For example, "you're-right" or "your-rope". Practice each word combination below.

You're reading →	☐ ☐ ☐ ☐ ☐
Your radio →	☐ ☐ ☐ ☐ ☐
You're right →	☐ ☐ ☐ ☐ ☐
Your robot →	☐ ☐ ☐ ☐ ☐
You're ready →	☐ ☐ ☐ ☐ ☐
Your reasons →	☐ ☐ ☐ ☐ ☐

I CAN SAY THE R SOUND!

You're ready to practice the R sound!

Sliding into an initial R from a final vocalic R can help you say it correctly. Say the first word and connect it to the second word. For example, "your-radio" or "you're-right". Practice each word combination below.

Did you finish your reading assignments?

Did you get your radio from Sam?

I believe you're right about that.

I saw your robot in the science fair.

I hope you're ready to have some fun.

You have your reasons for choosing that.

RL WORDS

Words that have the RL sound at the end can be particularly challenging for many students. It can be helpful to break down the tongue movements and slowly move from the ER sound to the L sound when initially targeting this sound combination.

Say the ER sound in isolation.

Slide the tongue tip forward to the alveolar ridge for production of L.

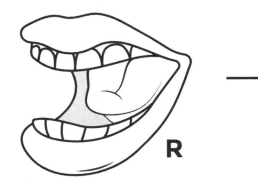

R

L

Do this slowly, and it will sound like you are saying the name Earl. Practice saying the word EARL, checking a box for each production.

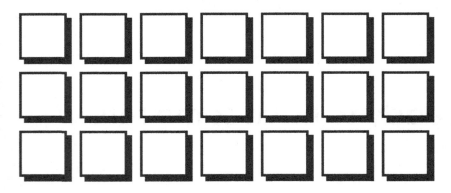

*If your client is not yet stimulable for the ER sound, you may want to try working on LR words before RL words. See page 25 for a helpful elicitation technique!

RL WORDS

Words that have the RL sound at the end can be particularly challenging for many students. It can be helpful to break down the tongue movements and slowly move from the ER sound to the L sound when initially targeting this sound combination.

Say the ER sound in isolation.

Slide the tongue tip forward to the alveolar ridge for production of L.

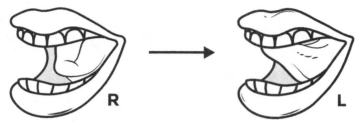

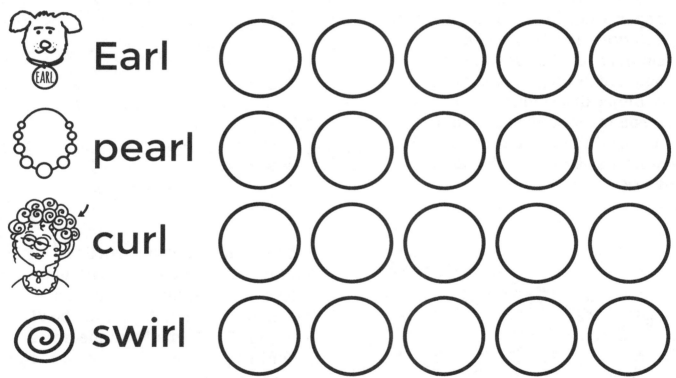

Earl

pearl

curl

swirl

girl

*If your client is not yet stimulable for the ER sound, you may want to try working on LR words before RL words. See page 25 for a helpful elicitation technique!

AUDITORY DISCRIMINATION

It is important for your student/client to be able to hear the difference between an accurate and inaccurate R sound. The next few pages focus on auditory discrimination.

On this page, instruct your client to say the sound and then decide if they produced it correctly or incorrectly. They will mark their answer on the page. You will be keeping track of their ability to discriminate between correct and incorrect productions. I recommend discreetly marking your notes on a scrap piece of paper. Once they've completed the activity, take the paper and complete the bottom section yourself. If they have poor auditory discrimination, I recommend working on this using minimal pairs for a couple sessions before starting drill work.

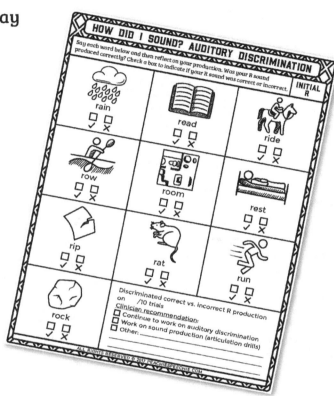

On this page, you will practice auditory discrimination with your client. For each set of words, you will say either the R word or the W word for five trials. Your client will color in a picture to show what they heard. For example, if you say, "ring, wing, ring, ring, wing", their paper would ideally look like this at the end of that trial:

HOW DID I SOUND? AUDITORY DISCRIMINATION

Say each word below and then reflect on your production. Was your R sound produced correctly? Check a box to indicate if your R sound was correct or incorrect.

INITIAL R

rain ☐✓ ☐✗	read ☐✓ ☐✗	ride ☐✓ ☐✗
row ☐✓ ☐✗	room ☐✓ ☐✗	rest ☐✓ ☐✗
rip ☐✓ ☐✗	rat ☐✓ ☐✗	run ☐✓ ☐✗

rock ☐✓ ☐✗

Discriminated correct vs. incorrect R production on ___ /10 trials

<u>Clinician recommendation</u>:
☐ Continue to work on auditory discrimination
☐ Work on sound production (articulation drills)
☐ Other: _____

_____

_____

HOW DID I SOUND? AUDITORY DISCRIMINATION

Say each word below and then reflect on your production. Was your R sound produced correctly? Check a box to indicate if your R sound was correct or incorrect.

MEDIAL R

person ☐✓ ☐✗	barn ☐✓ ☐✗	cart ☐✓ ☐✗
hero ☐✓ ☐✗	cereal ☐✓ ☐✗	siren ☐✓ ☐✗
firewood ☐✓ ☐✗	morning ☐✓ ☐✗	parrot ☐✓ ☐✗

married ☐✓ ☐✗

Discriminated correct vs. incorrect R production on ___/10 trials

Clinician recommendation:
☐ Continue to work on auditory discrimination
☐ Work on sound production (articulation drills)
☐ Other: _____
_____
_____

63

HOW DID I SOUND? AUDITORY DISCRIMINATION

Say each word below and then reflect on your production. Was your R sound produced correctly? Check a box to indicate if your R sound was correct or incorrect.

FINAL R

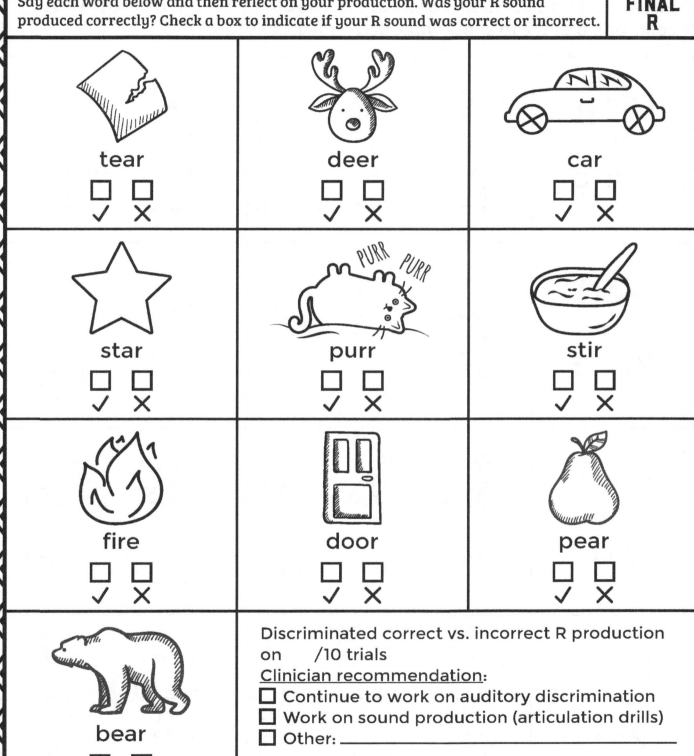

tear ☐✓ ☐✗

deer ☐✓ ☐✗

car ☐✓ ☐✗

star ☐✓ ☐✗

purr ☐✓ ☐✗

stir ☐✓ ☐✗

fire ☐✓ ☐✗

door ☐✓ ☐✗

pear ☐✓ ☐✗

bear ☐✓ ☐✗

Discriminated correct vs. incorrect R production on ___ /10 trials

<u>Clinician recommendation</u>:
☐ Continue to work on auditory discrimination
☐ Work on sound production (articulation drills)
☐ Other: _____

ALL RIGHTS RESERVED © 2017 PEACHIESPEECHIE.COM

AUDITORY DISCRIMINATION: R VS. W

Listen as your SLP/helper says the words aloud. As you hear the word, color one picture to show what you heard.

Ring or Wing					
Red or Wed					
Ride or Wide					
Rich or Witch					

AUDITORY DISCRIMINATION: R VS. W

Listen as your SLP/helper says the words aloud. As you hear the word, color one picture to show what you heard.

Rock or Walk	 
Rail or Whale	
Run or One	
Rest or West	

I CAN SAY THE R SOUND!

R Drill Practice

Now that you know how to position your tongue to say the R sound, let's practice! Practice getting your tongue into the correct position and producing the R sound. (Tip: Use a mirror to help if needed!) Color one of the letters below each time you practice.

I CAN SAY THE R SOUND!

Super Star Speech

Practice saying your R sound with your speech-language pathologist. For every 5 tries, color in a star on the sheet below. You are a Speech Super Star!

I CAN SAY THE R SOUND!

R Street

Use your finger (or a small car or other toy/object) to trace along the road. Every time you get to a sign, stop and practice your R sound 5 times.

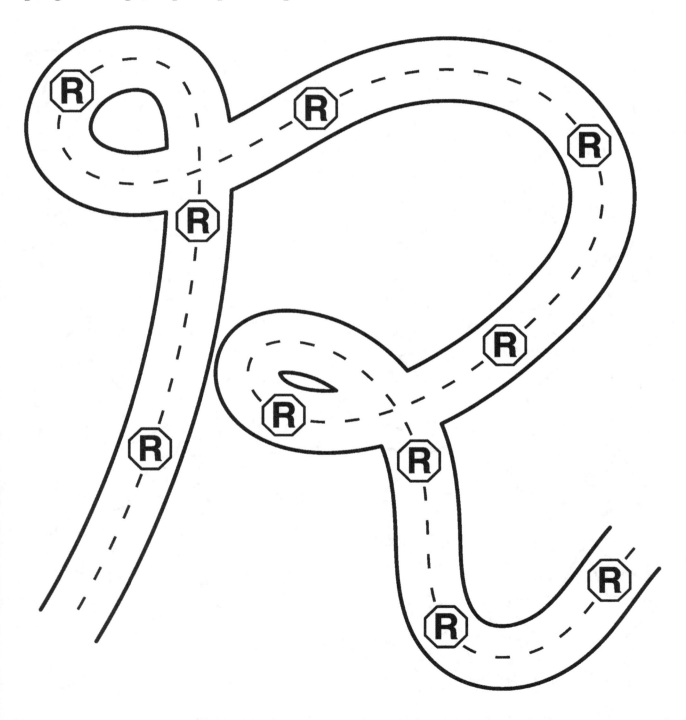

I CAN SAY THE R SOUND!

Minimal Pairs

Listen as your SLP/helper reads the sets of words below. Can you hear the difference between the R sound and the W sound? Point to the picture of the words you hear. Then, cut out the cards and practice saying the words yourself!

MINIMAL PAIRS: R VS. W DRILLS

Practice your R sound by saying the words below. You will switch between saying the R sound and the W sound at the beginning of the words. Pay attention to how your mouth changes as you say each word.

red wed red wed red wed red wed

rock walk rock walk rock walk rock walk

ring wing ring wing ring wing ring wing

rake wake rake wake rake wake rake wake

ride wide ride wide ride wide ride wide

MINIMAL PAIRS: R VS. W DRILLS

Practice your R sound by saying the words below. You will switch between saying the R sound and the W sound at the beginning of the words. Pay attention to how your mouth changes as you say each word.

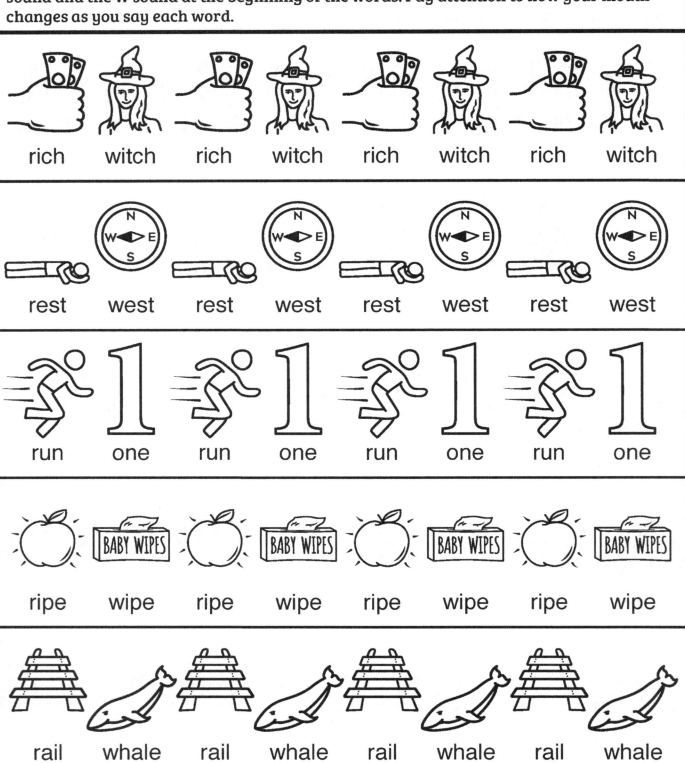

| rich | witch | rich | witch | rich | witch | rich | witch |

| rest | west | rest | west | rest | west | rest | west |

| run | one | run | one | run | one | run | one |

| ripe | wipe | ripe | wipe | ripe | wipe | ripe | wipe |

| rail | whale | rail | whale | rail | whale | rail | whale |

CONTRASTING PHONEMES: R VS. W

Read each sentence below and complete it by saying the R word on the right. Be sure to use your best R sound. If you say the W sound instead, the sentence won't make sense.

My favorite color is _____.

WED

RED

I found a _____ in the forest.

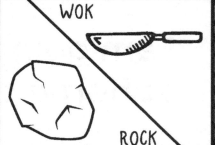

WOK

ROCK

Put the _____ on your finger.

WING

RING

I will _____ the leaves.

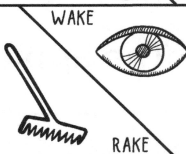

WAKE

RAKE

Can you _____ a bicycle?

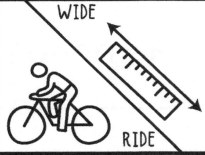

WIDE

RIDE

CONTRASTING PHONEMES: R VS. W

Read each sentence below and complete it by saying the R word on the right. Be sure to use your best R sound. If you say the W sound instead, the sentence won't make sense.

The _____ man lives in an expensive castle.	WITCH / RICH
I am going to _____ at home this weekend.	WEST / REST
She likes to _____ down the street.	ONE / RUN
The apples are _____ and juicy.	WIPE / RIPE
He needs a new fishing _____.	WHEEL / REEL

I CAN SAY THE R SOUND!

COARTICULATION TO FACILITATE PRODUCTION OF VOCALIC R

Coarticulation refers to the production of sounds being influenced by the sounds around it. The phonetic context of a sound can facilitate correct production of the sound (Bernthal, Bankson & Flipsen, 2009) and this is useful when working on the R sound.

Example:

When someone can produce the initial R sound in words (red, ripe, rest, etc.), but has difficulty achieving accurate production of final vocalic R (car, fur, bear, etc.), pairing the words together can facilitate production of the final R sound. This happens because you are anticipating production of the initial R sound and moving your tongue into the correct position.

Instead of practicing the word "her" by itself, I would try practicing it before the word "ring" and instruct my student/client to slide the words together ("herrr-ring"). From there, I would have them say the word "her" and then whisper the word "ring" and eventually fade away the word "ring" as they learned to produce the word "her" by itself.

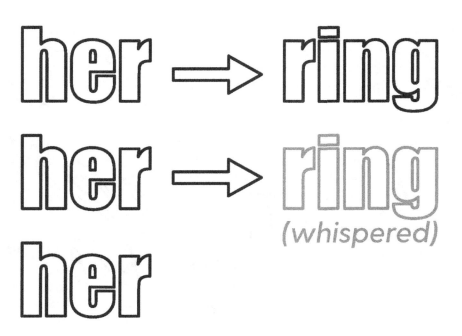

her → ring

her → ring (whispered)

her

I CAN SAY THE R SOUND!

Sliding into an initial R from a final vocalic R can help you say it correctly. Say the word "her" and then connect it to another word in the web. For example, "herrr-ring" or "herrr-rock". Practice each word combination below.

ER

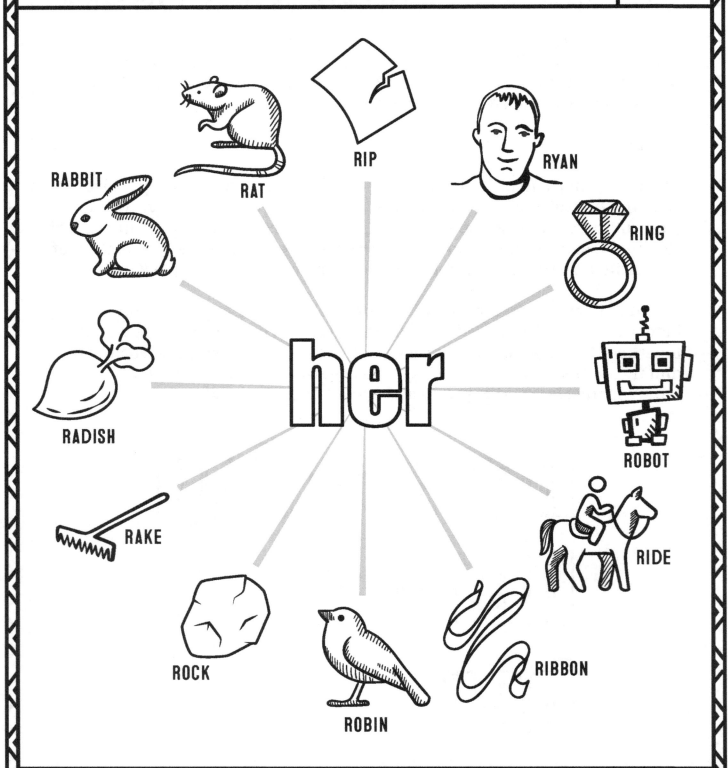

RAT

RIP

RYAN

RABBIT

RING

RADISH

ROBOT

her

RAKE

RIDE

ROCK

ROBIN

RIBBON

I CAN SAY THE R SOUND!

Sliding into an initial R from a final vocalic R can help you say it correctly. Say the word "car" and then connect it to another word in the web. For example, "carrr-ride" or "carrr-red". Practice each word combination below.

AR

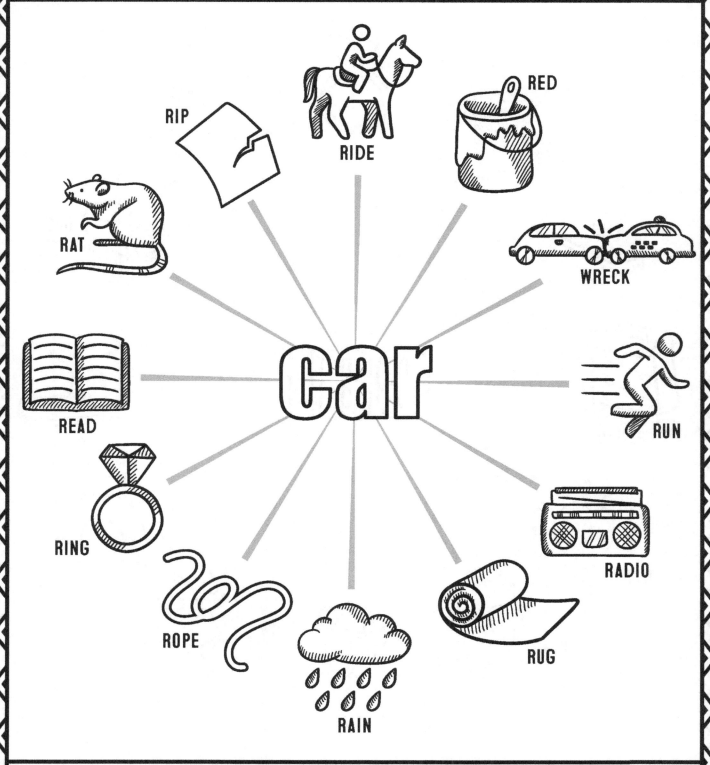

RIP

RIDE

RED

RAT

WRECK

READ

car

RUN

RING

RADIO

ROPE

RUG

RAIN

I CAN SAY THE R SOUND!

Sliding into an initial R from a final vocalic R can help you say it correctly. Say the word "ear" and then connect it to another word in the web. For example, "earrr-ring" or "earrr-rat". Practice each word combination below.

EAR

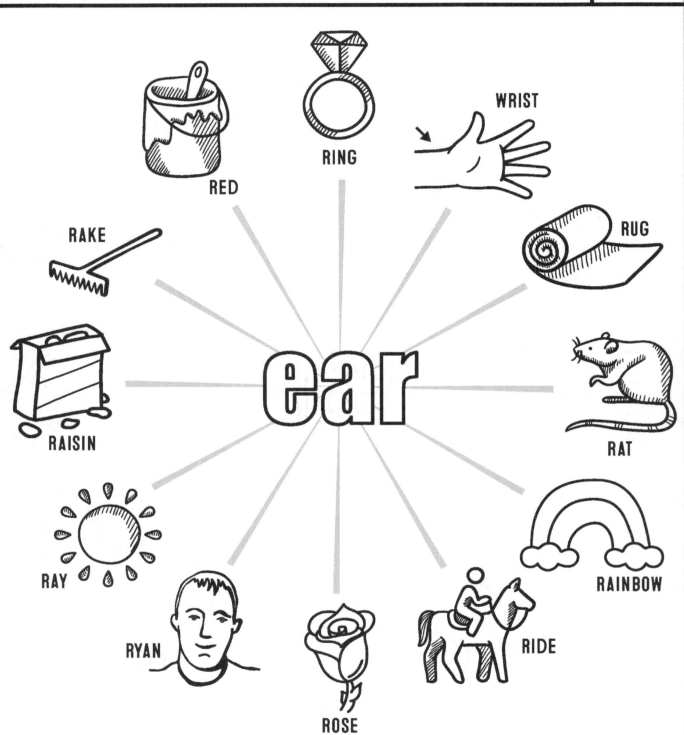

RED

RING

WRIST

RAKE

RUG

RAISIN

ear

RAT

RAY

RYAN

ROSE

RIDE

RAINBOW

I CAN SAY THE R SOUND!

Sliding into an initial R from a final vocalic R can help you say it correctly. Say the word "fire" and then connect it to another word in the web. For example, "firrre-rocket" or "firrre-ride". Practice each word combination below.

IRE

RIDE

RACE

RIGHT

ROW

READ

ROOF

RED

RICE

ROCKET

REEF

RICK

ROAST

I CAN SAY THE R SOUND!

Sliding into an initial R from a final vocalic R can help you say it correctly. Say the word "bear" and then connect it to another word in the web. For example, "bearrr-run" or "bearrr-rest". Practice each word combination below.

AIR

RED

RUN

ROPE

RIP

RAKE

bear

ROYAL

RAISINS

RAIN

ROBIN

REST

RUG

RIBBON

I CAN SAY THE R SOUND!

Sliding into an initial R from a final vocalic R can help you say it correctly. Say the word "more" and then connect it to another word in the web. For example, "morrre-red" or "morrre-rain". Practice each word combination below.

OR

RAIN

RICE

RED

RIP

RIBBON

RAISINS

ROOM

REST

RADIO

RABBIT

RAINBOW

READING

I CAN SAY THE R SOUND!

Facilitating Contexts for the R Sound

Sliding into an initial R from a final vocalic R can help you say it correctly. Say the first word and connect it to the second word. For example, "herrr-rope" or "stirrr-red". Practice each word combination below.

ER

HER ⟹ ROPE ☐ ☐ ☐ ☐ ☐

STIR ⟹ RED ☐ ☐ ☐ ☐ ☐

FUR ⟹ RIBBON ☐ ☐ ☐ ☐ ☐

SIR ⟹ READY ☐ ☐ ☐ ☐ ☐

PURR ⟹ ROSE ☐ ☐ ☐ ☐ ☐

I CAN SAY THE R SOUND!

Facilitating Contexts for the R Sound

Sliding into an initial R from a final vocalic R can help you say it correctly. Say the first word and connect it to the second word. For example, "carrr-red" or "starrr-race". Practice each word combination below.

AR

CAR ⟹ RED ☐ ☐ ☐ ☐ ☐

STAR ⟹ RACE ☐ ☐ ☐ ☐ ☐

FAR ⟹ RUN ☐ ☐ ☐ ☐ ☐

BAR ⟹ ROPE ☐ ☐ ☐ ☐ ☐

TAR ⟹ RAIN ☐ ☐ ☐ ☐ ☐

I CAN SAY THE R SOUND!

Facilitating Contexts for the R Sound

Sliding into an initial R from a final vocalic R can help you say it correctly. Say the first word and connect it to the second word. For example, "earrr-ring" or "fearrr-rent". Practice each word combination below.

EAR

EAR ⟹ RING ☐ ☐ ☐ ☐ ☐

FEAR ⟹ RENT ☐ ☐ ☐ ☐ ☐

PEER ⟹ REECE ☐ ☐ ☐ ☐ ☐

NEAR ⟹ RAT ☐ ☐ ☐ ☐ ☐

HEAR ⟹ RISE ☐ ☐ ☐ ☐ ☐

I CAN SAY THE R SOUND!

Facilitating Contexts for the R Sound

Sliding into an initial R from a final vocalic R can help you say it correctly. Say the first word and connect it to the second word. For example, "firrre-ring" or "wirrre-reach". Practice each word combination below.

IRE

FIRE ⇒ RING ☐ ☐ ☐ ☐ ☐

WIRE ⇒ REACH ☐ ☐ ☐ ☐ ☐

TIRE ⇒ RYAN ☐ ☐ ☐ ☐ ☐

ADMIRE ⇒ RIP ☐ ☐ ☐ ☐ ☐

LIAR ⇒ RIDE ☐ ☐ ☐ ☐ ☐

I CAN SAY THE R SOUND!

Facilitating Contexts for the R Sound

Sliding into an initial R from a final vocalic R can help you say it correctly. Say the first word and connect it to the second word. For example, "airrr-room" or "fairrr-rocket". Practice each word combination below.

AIR

AIR → ROOM ☐ ☐ ☐ ☐ ☐

FAIR → ROCKET ☐ ☐ ☐ ☐ ☐

TEAR → RAKE ☐ ☐ ☐ ☐ ☐

WEAR → RADISH ☐ ☐ ☐ ☐ ☐

PEAR → RAISIN ☐ ☐ ☐ ☐ ☐

I CAN SAY THE R SOUND!

Facilitating Contexts for the R Sound

Sliding into an initial R from a final vocalic R can help you say it correctly. Say the first word and connect it to the second word. For example, "sorrre-roast" or "pourrr-rice". Practice each word combination below.

OR

SORE ⟹ ROAST ☐ ☐ ☐ ☐ ☐

POUR ⟹ RICE ☐ ☐ ☐ ☐ ☐

TORE ⟹ READ ☐ ☐ ☐ ☐ ☐

MORE ⟹ RIBBON ☐ ☐ ☐ ☐ ☐

STORE ⟹ RIGHT ☐ ☐ ☐ ☐ ☐

I CAN SAY THE R SOUND!

Ray

A ray of sun

Ree

My name is Ree

Rye

Rye bread is tasty

Row

Row your boat

Roo

Little Roo is in a pouch

a e i o u

SOUND BY SOUND™ R SOUND PRACTICE

Focus on how your tongue and lips move as you say each sound in the words below. Remember to keep your tongue high and tense as you say the R sound. Practice each word five times.	INITIAL R
## RACE   	
## RUN   	
## RAT   	
## RIP   	

SOUND BY SOUND™ R SOUND PRACTICE

Focus on how your tongue and lips move as you say each sound in the words below. Remember to keep your tongue high and tense as you say the R sound. Practice each word five times.	INITIAL R
## ROAD   	
## RED 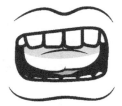  	
## ROCK   	
## RICH   	

SOUND BY SOUND™ R SOUND PRACTICE

Focus on how your tongue and lips move as you say each sound in the words below. Remember to keep your tongue high and tense as you say the R sound. Practice each word five times.

INITIAL R

ROOM

RING

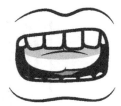   

ROPE

RAIN

SOUND BY SOUND™ R SOUND PRACTICE

Focus on how your tongue and lips move as you say each sound in the words below. Remember to keep your tongue high and tense as you say the R sound. Practice each word five times.	INITIAL ER
## EARN  	
## EARTH 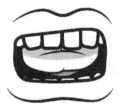 	
## EARL  	
## EARLY   	

SOUND BY SOUND™ R SOUND PRACTICE

Focus on how your tongue and lips move as you say each sound in the words below. Remember to keep your tongue high and tense as you say the R sound. Practice each word five times.

MEDIAL ER

LEARN

GIRL

TURN

 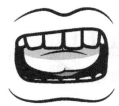  

FIRST

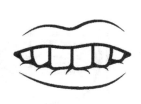    

SOUND BY SOUND™ R SOUND PRACTICE

Focus on how your tongue and lips move as you say each sound in the words below. Remember to keep your tongue high and tense as you say the R sound. Practice each word five times.	**FINAL ER**
FUR 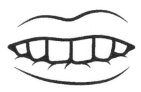 	
HER  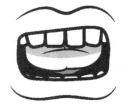	
PURR  	
STIR   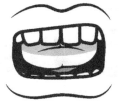	

SOUND BY SOUND™ R SOUND PRACTICE

Focus on how your tongue and lips move as you say each sound in the words below. Remember to keep your tongue high and tense as you say the R sound. Practice each word five times.

INITIAL AR

ARM

ART

ARK

 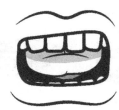 

ARCH

 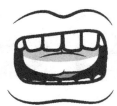 

SOUND BY SOUND™ R SOUND PRACTICE

Focus on how your tongue and lips move as you say each sound in the words below. Remember to keep your tongue high and tense as you say the R sound. Practice each word five times.	MEDIAL AR
## PARK    	
## BARN   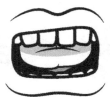 	
## CART   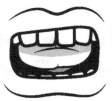 	
## MARK   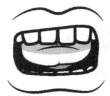 	

SOUND BY SOUND™ R SOUND PRACTICE

Focus on how your tongue and lips move as you say each sound in the words below. Remember to keep your tongue high and tense as you say the R sound. Practice each word five times.	**FINAL AR**
## CAR   	
## BAR   	
## STAR    	
## JAR   	

SOUND BY SOUND™ R SOUND PRACTICE

Focus on how your tongue and lips move as you say each sound in the words below. Remember to keep your tongue high and tense as you say the R sound. Practice each word five times.	INITIAL EAR
## EAR  	
## EARRING    	
## IRRITATE 	
## EERIE  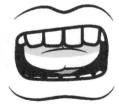 	

SOUND BY SOUND™ R SOUND PRACTICE

Focus on how your tongue and lips move as you say each sound in the words below. Remember to keep your tongue high and tense as you say the R sound. Practice each word five times.	**MEDIAL EAR**
## WEIRD    	
## BEARD   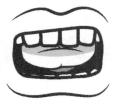 	
## HERO    	
## CEREAL 	

SOUND BY SOUND™ R SOUND PRACTICE

Focus on how your tongue and lips move as you say each sound in the words below. Remember to keep your tongue high and tense as you say the R sound. Practice each word five times.	**FINAL EAR**
HEAR   	
CHEER   	
FEAR 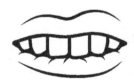  	
STEER    	

SOUND BY SOUND™ R SOUND PRACTICE

Focus on how your tongue and lips move as you say each sound in the words below. Remember to keep your tongue high and tense as you say the R sound. Practice each word five times.

INITIAL IRE

IRON

IRISH

IRELAND

IRENE
 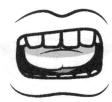 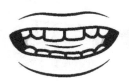  

SOUND BY SOUND™ R SOUND PRACTICE

Focus on how your tongue and lips move as you say each sound in the words below. Remember to keep your tongue high and tense as you say the R sound. Practice each word five times.	**MEDIAL IRE**
## TIRED    	
## PIRATE    	
## PLIERS    	
## TIRES   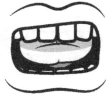 	

SOUND BY SOUND™ R SOUND PRACTICE

Focus on how your tongue and lips move as you say each sound in the words below. Remember to keep your tongue high and tense as you say the R sound. Practice each word five times.	**FINAL IRE**
## FIRE 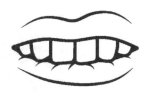  	
## WIRE   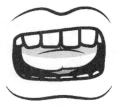	
## FLYER 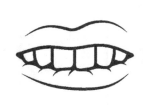   	
## CHOIR    	

SOUND BY SOUND™ R SOUND PRACTICE

Focus on how your tongue and lips move as you say each sound in the words below. Remember to keep your tongue high and tense as you say the R sound. Practice each word five times.	INITIAL AIR
## AIR  	
## ARROW   	
## AARON  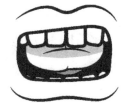  	
## AREA   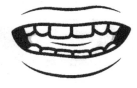 	

SOUND BY SOUND™ R SOUND PRACTICE

Focus on how your tongue and lips move as you say each sound in the words below. Remember to keep your tongue high and tense as you say the R sound. Practice each word five times.

MEDIAL AIR

CARROT

CHERRY

  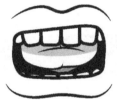  

HAIRY

STEREO

SOUND BY SOUND™ R SOUND PRACTICE

Focus on how your tongue and lips move as you say each sound in the words below. Remember to keep your tongue high and tense as you say the R sound. Practice each word five times.

FINAL AIR

THERE

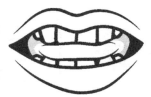  

HAIR

STARE

SHARE

SOUND BY SOUND™ R SOUND PRACTICE

Focus on how your tongue and lips move as you say each sound in the words below. Remember to keep your tongue high and tense as you say the R sound. Practice each word five times.

ORBIT

ORANGE

ORCHID

ORGAN

SOUND-BY-SOUND™ ALL RIGHTS RESERVED ©PEACHIESPEECHIE.COM

SOUND BY SOUND™ R SOUND PRACTICE

Focus on how your tongue and lips move as you say each sound in the words below. Remember to keep your tongue high and tense as you say the R sound. Practice each word five times.	MEDIAL OR
BOARD    	
STORY   	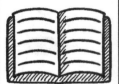
SHORT    	
THORN   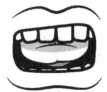 	

SOUND BY SOUND™ R SOUND PRACTICE

Focus on how your tongue and lips move as you say each sound in the words below. Remember to keep your tongue high and tense as you say the R sound. Practice each word five times.	**FINAL OR**
## POUR   	
## STORE    	
## FOUR 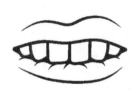  	
## TORE   	

SOUND BY SOUND™ R SOUND PRACTICE

Focus on how your tongue and lips move as you say each sound in the words below. Remember to keep your tongue high and tense as you say the R sound. Practice each word five times.	R BLENDS
CRAB    	
FROG 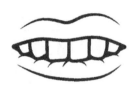 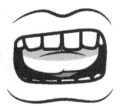  	
BRICK  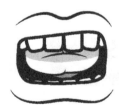  	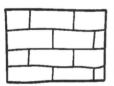
PRUNE    	

111

SOUND BY SOUND™ R SOUND PRACTICE

Focus on how your tongue and lips move as you say each sound in the words below. Remember to keep your tongue high and tense as you say the R sound. Practice each word five times.

R BLENDS

TREE

GROW

TRUCK

BREW
 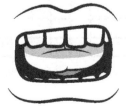  

SOUND BY SOUND™ DATA: R SOUND PRACTICE

This data sheet is designed to be used with the Sound-By-Sound pages for the R sound. Present the pages to your student and ask them to say the words on the pages. Provide models/prompts as appropriate for your student. Mark the grid below with + for accurate production and - for inaccurate production.

NAME:

Prevocalic /r/				
1. RACE				
2. RUN				
3. RAT				
4. RIP				
5. ROAD				
6. RED				
7. ROCK				
8. RICH				
9. ROOM				
10. RING				
11. ROPE				
12. RAIN				

R-Blends
13. TREE
14. GROW
15. CRAB
16. FROG
17. BRICK
18. PRUNE
19. TRUCK
20. BREW

AR words
21. ARM
22. ART
23. ARK
24. ARCH
25. PARK
26. BARN
27. CART
28. MARK
29. CAR
30. BAR

31. STAR
32. JAR

ER words
33. EARN
34. EARTH
35. EARL
36. EARLY
37. TURN
38. FIRST
39. LEARN
40. GIRL
41. FUR
42. HER
43. PURR
44. STIR

AIR words
45. AIR
46. ARROW
47. AARON
48. AREA
49. CARROT
50. CHERRY
51. HAIRY
52. STEREO
53. THERE
54. HAIR
55. STARE
56. SHARE

IRE words
57. IRON
58. IRISH
59. IRELAND
60. IRENE

61. TIRED
62. PIRATE
63. PLIERS
64. TIRES
65. FIRE
66. WIRE
67. FLYER
68. CHOIR

EAR words
69. EAR
70. EARRING
71. IRRITATE
72. EERIE
73. WEIRD
74. BEARD
75. HERO
76. CEREAL
77. HEAR
78. CHEER
79. FEAR
80. STEER

OR words
81. ORBIT
82. ORANGE
83. ORCHID
84. ORGAN
85. BOARD
86. STORY
87. SHORT
88. THORN
89. POUR
90. STORE
91. FOUR
92. TORE

NOTES:

I CAN SAY THE R SOUND!

Say the words below. Be sure to use your best R sound. Mark a box for every production. If you complete the entire worksheet, you will have practiced 100 times!

INITIAL R

Retroflexed R

Bunched R

- Pull your tongue back
- Keep it high
- Make it tense
- Turn your voice on

Race	☐ ☐ ☐ ☐ ☐ ☐ ☐ ☐ ☐ ☐
Radio	☐ ☐ ☐ ☐ ☐ ☐ ☐ ☐ ☐ ☐
Rain	☐ ☐ ☐ ☐ ☐ ☐ ☐ ☐ ☐ ☐
Raised	☐ ☐ ☐ ☐ ☐ ☐ ☐ ☐ ☐ ☐
Ran	☐ ☐ ☐ ☐ ☐ ☐ ☐ ☐ ☐ ☐
Reached	☐ ☐ ☐ ☐ ☐ ☐ ☐ ☐ ☐ ☐
Read	☐ ☐ ☐ ☐ ☐ ☐ ☐ ☐ ☐ ☐
Ready	☐ ☐ ☐ ☐ ☐ ☐ ☐ ☐ ☐ ☐
Real	☐ ☐ ☐ ☐ ☐ ☐ ☐ ☐ ☐ ☐
Reason	☐ ☐ ☐ ☐ ☐ ☐ ☐ ☐ ☐ ☐

The above target words are high frequency words, sight words and common nouns. These words were selected to support reading skills in addition to speech sound production. (Fry, 1997)

I CAN SAY THE R SOUND!

Say the words below. Be sure to use your best R sound. Mark a box for every production. If you complete the entire worksheet, you will have practiced 100 times!

INITIAL R

Retroflexed R

Bunched R

- Pull your tongue back
- Keep it high
- Make it tense
- Turn your voice on

Red	☐ ☐ ☐ ☐ ☐ ☐ ☐ ☐ ☐ ☐
Region	☐ ☐ ☐ ☐ ☐ ☐ ☐ ☐ ☐ ☐
Remain	☐ ☐ ☐ ☐ ☐ ☐ ☐ ☐ ☐ ☐
Repeated	☐ ☐ ☐ ☐ ☐ ☐ ☐ ☐ ☐ ☐
Report	☐ ☐ ☐ ☐ ☐ ☐ ☐ ☐ ☐ ☐
Rest	☐ ☐ ☐ ☐ ☐ ☐ ☐ ☐ ☐ ☐
Result	☐ ☐ ☐ ☐ ☐ ☐ ☐ ☐ ☐ ☐
Return	☐ ☐ ☐ ☐ ☐ ☐ ☐ ☐ ☐ ☐
Rich	☐ ☐ ☐ ☐ ☐ ☐ ☐ ☐ ☐ ☐
Ride	☐ ☐ ☐ ☐ ☐ ☐ ☐ ☐ ☐ ☐

The above target words are high frequency words, sight words and common nouns. These words were selected to support reading skills in addition to speech sound production. (Fry, 1997)

I CAN SAY THE R SOUND!

Say the words below. Be sure to use your best R sound. Mark a box for every production. If you complete the entire worksheet, you will have practiced 100 times!

INITIAL R

Retroflexed R

Bunched R

- Pull your tongue back
- Keep it high
- Make it tense
- Turn your voice on

Right	☐ ☐ ☐ ☐ ☐ ☐ ☐ ☐ ☐ ☐
Ring	☐ ☐ ☐ ☐ ☐ ☐ ☐ ☐ ☐ ☐
Rise	☐ ☐ ☐ ☐ ☐ ☐ ☐ ☐ ☐ ☐
Rock	☐ ☐ ☐ ☐ ☐ ☐ ☐ ☐ ☐ ☐
Room	☐ ☐ ☐ ☐ ☐ ☐ ☐ ☐ ☐ ☐
Round	☐ ☐ ☐ ☐ ☐ ☐ ☐ ☐ ☐ ☐
Row	☐ ☐ ☐ ☐ ☐ ☐ ☐ ☐ ☐ ☐
Road	☐ ☐ ☐ ☐ ☐ ☐ ☐ ☐ ☐ ☐
Rule	☐ ☐ ☐ ☐ ☐ ☐ ☐ ☐ ☐ ☐
Run	☐ ☐ ☐ ☐ ☐ ☐ ☐ ☐ ☐ ☐

The above target words are high frequency words, sight words and common nouns. These words were selected to support reading skills in addition to speech sound production. (Fry, 1997)

I CAN SAY THE R SOUND!

Say the words below. Be sure to use your best R sound. Mark a box for every production. If you complete the entire worksheet, you will have practiced 100 times!

MEDIAL R

Retroflexed R

Bunched R

- Pull your tongue back
- Keep it high
- Make it tense
- Turn your voice on

Dark	☐ ☐ ☐ ☐ ☐ ☐ ☐ ☐ ☐ ☐
Large	☐ ☐ ☐ ☐ ☐ ☐ ☐ ☐ ☐ ☐
Start	☐ ☐ ☐ ☐ ☐ ☐ ☐ ☐ ☐ ☐
Learn	☐ ☐ ☐ ☐ ☐ ☐ ☐ ☐ ☐ ☐
Person	☐ ☐ ☐ ☐ ☐ ☐ ☐ ☐ ☐ ☐
Carry	☐ ☐ ☐ ☐ ☐ ☐ ☐ ☐ ☐ ☐
Paragraph	☐ ☐ ☐ ☐ ☐ ☐ ☐ ☐ ☐ ☐
Story	☐ ☐ ☐ ☐ ☐ ☐ ☐ ☐ ☐ ☐
Morning	☐ ☐ ☐ ☐ ☐ ☐ ☐ ☐ ☐ ☐
Period	☐ ☐ ☐ ☐ ☐ ☐ ☐ ☐ ☐ ☐

I CAN SAY THE R SOUND!

Say the words below. Be sure to use your best R sound. Mark a box for every production. If you complete the entire worksheet, you will have practiced 100 times!

FINAL R

Retroflexed R

Bunched R

- Pull your tongue back
- Keep it high
- Make it tense
- Turn your voice on

Car	☐ ☐ ☐ ☐ ☐ ☐ ☐ ☐ ☐ ☐
Far	☐ ☐ ☐ ☐ ☐ ☐ ☐ ☐ ☐ ☐
Her	☐ ☐ ☐ ☐ ☐ ☐ ☐ ☐ ☐ ☐
Number	☐ ☐ ☐ ☐ ☐ ☐ ☐ ☐ ☐ ☐
Year	☐ ☐ ☐ ☐ ☐ ☐ ☐ ☐ ☐ ☐
Near	☐ ☐ ☐ ☐ ☐ ☐ ☐ ☐ ☐ ☐
Pair	☐ ☐ ☐ ☐ ☐ ☐ ☐ ☐ ☐ ☐
Where	☐ ☐ ☐ ☐ ☐ ☐ ☐ ☐ ☐ ☐
For	☐ ☐ ☐ ☐ ☐ ☐ ☐ ☐ ☐ ☐
Store	☐ ☐ ☐ ☐ ☐ ☐ ☐ ☐ ☐ ☐

I CAN SAY THE R SOUND!

Say the words below. Be sure to use your best R sound. Mark a box for every production. If you complete the entire worksheet, you will have practiced 100 times!

ER WORDS

Retroflexed R

Bunched R

- Pull your tongue back
- Keep it high
- Make it tense
- Turn your voice on

Earth	☐ ☐ ☐ ☐ ☐ ☐ ☐ ☐ ☐ ☐
Early	☐ ☐ ☐ ☐ ☐ ☐ ☐ ☐ ☐ ☐
Either	☐ ☐ ☐ ☐ ☐ ☐ ☐ ☐ ☐ ☐
Exercise	☐ ☐ ☐ ☐ ☐ ☐ ☐ ☐ ☐ ☐
First	☐ ☐ ☐ ☐ ☐ ☐ ☐ ☐ ☐ ☐
Flowers	☐ ☐ ☐ ☐ ☐ ☐ ☐ ☐ ☐ ☐
Finger	☐ ☐ ☐ ☐ ☐ ☐ ☐ ☐ ☐ ☐
Heard	☐ ☐ ☐ ☐ ☐ ☐ ☐ ☐ ☐ ☐
Her	☐ ☐ ☐ ☐ ☐ ☐ ☐ ☐ ☐ ☐
Hours	☐ ☐ ☐ ☐ ☐ ☐ ☐ ☐ ☐ ☐

The above target words are high frequency words, sight words and common nouns. These words were selected to support reading skills in addition to speech sound production. (Fry, 1997)

I CAN SAY THE R SOUND!

Say the words below. Be sure to use your best R sound. Mark a box for every production. If you complete the entire worksheet, you will have practiced 100 times!

ER WORDS

Retroflexed R

Bunched R

- Pull your tongue back
- Keep it high
- Make it tense
- Turn your voice on

However	☐	☐	☐	☐	☐	☐	☐	☐	☐	☐
Learn	☐	☐	☐	☐	☐	☐	☐	☐	☐	☐
Letter	☐	☐	☐	☐	☐	☐	☐	☐	☐	☐
Major	☐	☐	☐	☐	☐	☐	☐	☐	☐	☐
Matter	☐	☐	☐	☐	☐	☐	☐	☐	☐	☐
Measure	☐	☐	☐	☐	☐	☐	☐	☐	☐	☐
Modern	☐	☐	☐	☐	☐	☐	☐	☐	☐	☐
Mother	☐	☐	☐	☐	☐	☐	☐	☐	☐	☐
Never	☐	☐	☐	☐	☐	☐	☐	☐	☐	☐
Number	☐	☐	☐	☐	☐	☐	☐	☐	☐	☐

The above target words are high frequency words, sight words and common nouns. These words were selected to support reading skills in addition to speech sound production. (Fry, 1997)

I CAN SAY THE R SOUND!

Say the words below. Be sure to use your best R sound. Mark a box for every production. If you complete the entire worksheet, you will have practiced 100 times!

ER WORDS

Retroflexed R

Bunched R

- Pull your tongue back
- Keep it high
- Make it tense
- Turn your voice on

Other	☐ ☐ ☐ ☐ ☐ ☐ ☐ ☐ ☐ ☐
Over	☐ ☐ ☐ ☐ ☐ ☐ ☐ ☐ ☐ ☐
Paper	☐ ☐ ☐ ☐ ☐ ☐ ☐ ☐ ☐ ☐
Perhaps	☐ ☐ ☐ ☐ ☐ ☐ ☐ ☐ ☐ ☐
Person	☐ ☐ ☐ ☐ ☐ ☐ ☐ ☐ ☐ ☐
Summer	☐ ☐ ☐ ☐ ☐ ☐ ☐ ☐ ☐ ☐
Surface	☐ ☐ ☐ ☐ ☐ ☐ ☐ ☐ ☐ ☐
Teacher	☐ ☐ ☐ ☐ ☐ ☐ ☐ ☐ ☐ ☐
Water	☐ ☐ ☐ ☐ ☐ ☐ ☐ ☐ ☐ ☐
Weather	☐ ☐ ☐ ☐ ☐ ☐ ☐ ☐ ☐ ☐

The above target words are high frequency words, sight words and common nouns. These words were selected to support reading skills in addition to speech sound production. (Fry, 1997)

I CAN SAY THE R SOUND!

Say the words below. Be sure to use your best R sound. Mark a box for every production. If you complete the entire worksheet, you will have practiced 100 times!

AR WORDS

Arm	☐ ☐ ☐ ☐ ☐ ☐ ☐ ☐ ☐ ☐
Art	☐ ☐ ☐ ☐ ☐ ☐ ☐ ☐ ☐ ☐
Dark	☐ ☐ ☐ ☐ ☐ ☐ ☐ ☐ ☐ ☐
Hard	☐ ☐ ☐ ☐ ☐ ☐ ☐ ☐ ☐ ☐
Large	☐ ☐ ☐ ☐ ☐ ☐ ☐ ☐ ☐ ☐
Park	☐ ☐ ☐ ☐ ☐ ☐ ☐ ☐ ☐ ☐
Sharp	☐ ☐ ☐ ☐ ☐ ☐ ☐ ☐ ☐ ☐
Start	☐ ☐ ☐ ☐ ☐ ☐ ☐ ☐ ☐ ☐
Far	☐ ☐ ☐ ☐ ☐ ☐ ☐ ☐ ☐ ☐
Car	☐ ☐ ☐ ☐ ☐ ☐ ☐ ☐ ☐ ☐

The above target words are high frequency words, sight words and common nouns. These words were selected to support reading skills in addition to speech sound production. (Fry, 1997)

I CAN SAY THE R SOUND!

Say the words below. Be sure to use your best R sound. Mark a box for every production. If you complete the entire worksheet, you will have practiced 100 times!

EAR WORDS

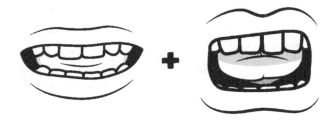

Appear	☐	☐	☐	☐	☐	☐	☐	☐	☐	☐
Ears	☐	☐	☐	☐	☐	☐	☐	☐	☐	☐
Experience	☐	☐	☐	☐	☐	☐	☐	☐	☐	☐
Fear	☐	☐	☐	☐	☐	☐	☐	☐	☐	☐
Hear	☐	☐	☐	☐	☐	☐	☐	☐	☐	☐
Material	☐	☐	☐	☐	☐	☐	☐	☐	☐	☐
Near	☐	☐	☐	☐	☐	☐	☐	☐	☐	☐
Period	☐	☐	☐	☐	☐	☐	☐	☐	☐	☐
Year	☐	☐	☐	☐	☐	☐	☐	☐	☐	☐
Dear	☐	☐	☐	☐	☐	☐	☐	☐	☐	☐

I CAN SAY THE R SOUND!

Say the words below. Be sure to use your best R sound. Mark a box for every production. If you complete the entire worksheet, you will have practiced 100 times!

IRE WORDS

Irish	☐ ☐ ☐ ☐ ☐ ☐ ☐ ☐ ☐ ☐
Iris	☐ ☐ ☐ ☐ ☐ ☐ ☐ ☐ ☐ ☐
Irene	☐ ☐ ☐ ☐ ☐ ☐ ☐ ☐ ☐ ☐
Tired	☐ ☐ ☐ ☐ ☐ ☐ ☐ ☐ ☐ ☐
Siren	☐ ☐ ☐ ☐ ☐ ☐ ☐ ☐ ☐ ☐
Pliers	☐ ☐ ☐ ☐ ☐ ☐ ☐ ☐ ☐ ☐
Fire	☐ ☐ ☐ ☐ ☐ ☐ ☐ ☐ ☐ ☐
Wire	☐ ☐ ☐ ☐ ☐ ☐ ☐ ☐ ☐ ☐
Tire	☐ ☐ ☐ ☐ ☐ ☐ ☐ ☐ ☐ ☐
Entire	☐ ☐ ☐ ☐ ☐ ☐ ☐ ☐ ☐ ☐

I CAN SAY THE R SOUND!

Say the words below. Be sure to use your best R sound. Mark a box for every production. If you complete the entire worksheet, you will have practiced 100 times!

AIR WORDS

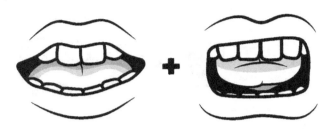

Air	☐ ☐ ☐ ☐ ☐ ☐ ☐ ☐ ☐ ☐
Care	☐ ☐ ☐ ☐ ☐ ☐ ☐ ☐ ☐ ☐
Carry	☐ ☐ ☐ ☐ ☐ ☐ ☐ ☐ ☐ ☐
Fair	☐ ☐ ☐ ☐ ☐ ☐ ☐ ☐ ☐ ☐
Hair	☐ ☐ ☐ ☐ ☐ ☐ ☐ ☐ ☐ ☐
Pair	☐ ☐ ☐ ☐ ☐ ☐ ☐ ☐ ☐ ☐
Paragraph	☐ ☐ ☐ ☐ ☐ ☐ ☐ ☐ ☐ ☐
Square	☐ ☐ ☐ ☐ ☐ ☐ ☐ ☐ ☐ ☐
There	☐ ☐ ☐ ☐ ☐ ☐ ☐ ☐ ☐ ☐
Where	☐ ☐ ☐ ☐ ☐ ☐ ☐ ☐ ☐ ☐

125

I CAN SAY THE R SOUND!

Say the words below. Be sure to use your best R sound. Mark a box for every production. If you complete the entire worksheet, you will have practiced 100 times!

OR WORDS

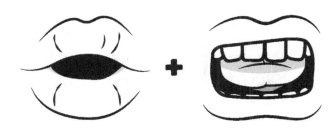

Corn	☐ ☐ ☐ ☐ ☐ ☐ ☐ ☐ ☐ ☐
Force	☐ ☐ ☐ ☐ ☐ ☐ ☐ ☐ ☐ ☐
Four	☐ ☐ ☐ ☐ ☐ ☐ ☐ ☐ ☐ ☐
Horse	☐ ☐ ☐ ☐ ☐ ☐ ☐ ☐ ☐ ☐
Morning	☐ ☐ ☐ ☐ ☐ ☐ ☐ ☐ ☐ ☐
North	☐ ☐ ☐ ☐ ☐ ☐ ☐ ☐ ☐ ☐
Poor	☐ ☐ ☐ ☐ ☐ ☐ ☐ ☐ ☐ ☐
Score	☐ ☐ ☐ ☐ ☐ ☐ ☐ ☐ ☐ ☐
Store	☐ ☐ ☐ ☐ ☐ ☐ ☐ ☐ ☐ ☐
Story	☐ ☐ ☐ ☐ ☐ ☐ ☐ ☐ ☐ ☐

I CAN SAY THE R SOUND!

Say the words below. Be sure to use your best R sound. Mark a box for every production. If you complete the entire worksheet, you will have practiced 100 times!

R BLENDS

+ 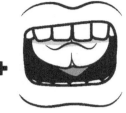 + 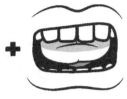 Say your R sound and its partner sound to make a consonant blend.

Retroflexed R   **Bunched R**

Create	☐ ☐ ☐ ☐ ☐ ☐ ☐ ☐ ☐ ☐
Cry	☐ ☐ ☐ ☐ ☐ ☐ ☐ ☐ ☐ ☐
From	☐ ☐ ☐ ☐ ☐ ☐ ☐ ☐ ☐ ☐
Tree	☐ ☐ ☐ ☐ ☐ ☐ ☐ ☐ ☐ ☐
Fruit	☐ ☐ ☐ ☐ ☐ ☐ ☐ ☐ ☐ ☐
Draw	☐ ☐ ☐ ☐ ☐ ☐ ☐ ☐ ☐ ☐
Dress	☐ ☐ ☐ ☐ ☐ ☐ ☐ ☐ ☐ ☐
Grew	☐ ☐ ☐ ☐ ☐ ☐ ☐ ☐ ☐ ☐
Ground	☐ ☐ ☐ ☐ ☐ ☐ ☐ ☐ ☐ ☐
Problem	☐ ☐ ☐ ☐ ☐ ☐ ☐ ☐ ☐ ☐

The above target words are high frequency words, sight words and common nouns. These words were selected to support reading skills in addition to speech sound production. (Fry, 1997)

I CAN SAY THE R SOUND!

Say the words below. Be sure to use your best R sound. Mark a box for every production. If you complete the entire worksheet, you will have practiced 100 times!

R BLENDS

+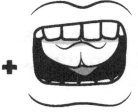

Retroflexed R

+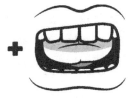

Bunched R

Say your R sound and its partner sound to make a consonant blend.

Free	☐ ☐ ☐ ☐ ☐ ☐ ☐ ☐ ☐ ☐
Friends	☐ ☐ ☐ ☐ ☐ ☐ ☐ ☐ ☐ ☐
Triangle	☐ ☐ ☐ ☐ ☐ ☐ ☐ ☐ ☐ ☐
Trouble	☐ ☐ ☐ ☐ ☐ ☐ ☐ ☐ ☐ ☐
Crops	☐ ☐ ☐ ☐ ☐ ☐ ☐ ☐ ☐ ☐
Cross	☐ ☐ ☐ ☐ ☐ ☐ ☐ ☐ ☐ ☐
Crowd	☐ ☐ ☐ ☐ ☐ ☐ ☐ ☐ ☐ ☐
Grass	☐ ☐ ☐ ☐ ☐ ☐ ☐ ☐ ☐ ☐
Green	☐ ☐ ☐ ☐ ☐ ☐ ☐ ☐ ☐ ☐
Pretty	☐ ☐ ☐ ☐ ☐ ☐ ☐ ☐ ☐ ☐

The above target words are high frequency words, sight words and common nouns. These words were selected to support reading skills in addition to speech sound production. (Fry, 1997)

I CAN SAY THE R SOUND!

Say the words below. Be sure to use your best R sound. Mark a box for every production. If you complete the entire worksheet, you will have practiced 100 times!

R BLENDS

+ 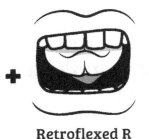 + 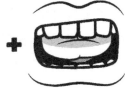 Say your R sound and its partner sound to make a consonant blend.

Retroflexed R   **Bunched R**

Group ☐ ☐ ☐ ☐ ☐ ☐ ☐ ☐ ☐ ☐

President ☐ ☐ ☐ ☐ ☐ ☐ ☐ ☐ ☐ ☐

Great ☐ ☐ ☐ ☐ ☐ ☐ ☐ ☐ ☐ ☐

Trip ☐ ☐ ☐ ☐ ☐ ☐ ☐ ☐ ☐ ☐

Drive ☐ ☐ ☐ ☐ ☐ ☐ ☐ ☐ ☐ ☐

Drop ☐ ☐ ☐ ☐ ☐ ☐ ☐ ☐ ☐ ☐

Dry ☐ ☐ ☐ ☐ ☐ ☐ ☐ ☐ ☐ ☐

Trade ☐ ☐ ☐ ☐ ☐ ☐ ☐ ☐ ☐ ☐

Train ☐ ☐ ☐ ☐ ☐ ☐ ☐ ☐ ☐ ☐

Front ☐ ☐ ☐ ☐ ☐ ☐ ☐ ☐ ☐ ☐

The above target words are high frequency words, sight words and common nouns. These words were selected to support reading skills in addition to speech sound production. (Fry, 1997)

I CAN SAY THE R SOUND!

Say and Dot: Initial R in Syllables

Mark the circles below as you practice the R sound in syllables.

Ray	Ree	Rye	Row	Roo
○	○	○	○	○
○	○	○	○	○
○	○	○	○	○
○	○	○	○	○
○	○	○	○	○
○	○	○	○	○
○	○	○	○	○
You did it!	You did it!	You did it!	You did it!	You did it!

I CAN SAY THE R SOUND!

Say and Dot: Initial R Words

Mark the circles below as you practice the R sound in words.

Rat	Rain	Roll	Run	Rip
◯	◯	◯	◯	◯
◯	◯	◯	◯	◯
◯	◯	◯	◯	◯
◯	◯	◯	◯	◯
◯	◯	◯	◯	◯
◯	◯	◯	◯	◯
◯	◯	◯	◯	◯
You did it!	You did it!	You did it!	You did it!	You did it!

I CAN SAY THE R SOUND!

Say and Dot: Initial R Words

Mark the circles below as you practice the R sound in words.

Robin	Ring	Write	Rick	Race

You did it! (×5)

I CAN SAY THE R SOUND!

Say and Dot: Initial R Words

Mark the circles below as you practice the R sound in words.

Rainbow	Radio	Rolling	Radish	Recycle

You did it! You did it! You did it! You did it! You did it!

I CAN SAY THE R SOUND!

Say and Dot: Initial ER Words

Mark the circles below as you practice the ER sound in words.

Ernie	Earnings	Irma	Earth	Early
○	○	○	○	○
○	○	○	○	○
○	○	○	○	○
○	○	○	○	○
○	○	○	○	○
○	○	○	○	○
○	○	○	○	○
You did it!	You did it!	You did it!	You did it!	You did it!

I CAN SAY THE R SOUND!

Say and Dot: Medial ER Words

Mark the circles below as you practice the ER sound in words.

Person	Turnip	Learn	Nervous	Furry
○	○	○	○	○
○	○	○	○	○
○	○	○	○	○
○	○	○	○	○
○	○	○	○	○
○	○	○	○	○
○	○	○	○	○
You did it!	You did it!	You did it!	You did it!	You did it!

I CAN SAY THE R SOUND!

Say and Dot: Final ER Words

Mark the circles below as you practice the ER sound in words.

Sir	Fur	Her	Purr	Stir

You did it! You did it! You did it! You did it! You did it!

I CAN SAY THE R SOUND!

Say and Dot: Initial AR Words

Mark the circles below as you practice the AR sound in words.

Army	Aardvark	Artwork	Artist	Argue

You did it! (×5)

I CAN SAY THE R SOUND!

Say and Dot: Medial AR Words

Mark the circles below as you practice the AR sound in words.

Barn	Carton	Farm	Cart	Martian

○	○	○	○	○
○	○	○	○	○
○	○	○	○	○
○	○	○	○	○
○	○	○	○	○
○	○	○	○	○
○	○	○	○	○

| You did it! | You did it! | You did it! | You did it! | You did it! |

I CAN SAY THE R SOUND!

Say and Dot: Final AR Words

Mark the circles below as you practice the AR sound in words.

Star	Jar	Car	Bar	Tar

You did it! | You did it! | You did it! | You did it! | You did it!

I CAN SAY THE R SOUND!

Say and Dot: Initial EAR Words

Mark the circles below as you practice the EAR sound in words.

Earrings	Irritated	Eerie	Ear lobe	Earphones
○	○	○	○	○
○	○	○	○	○
○	○	○	○	○
○	○	○	○	○
○	○	○	○	○
○	○	○	○	○
○	○	○	○	○
You did it!	You did it!	You did it!	You did it!	You did it!

I CAN SAY THE R SOUND!

Say and Dot: Medial EAR Words

Mark the circles below as you practice the EAR sound in words.

Hero	Cereal	Pierced	Beard	Cafeteria
○	○	○	○	○
○	○	○	○	○
○	○	○	○	○
○	○	○	○	○
○	○	○	○	○
○	○	○	○	○
○	○	○	○	○
You did it!	You did it!	You did it!	You did it!	You did it!

I CAN SAY THE R SOUND!

Say and Dot: Final EAR Words

Mark the circles below as you practice the EAR sound in words.

New Year	Tear	Mountaineer	Deer	Fear
○	○	○	○	○
○	○	○	○	○
○	○	○	○	○
○	○	○	○	○
○	○	○	○	○
○	○	○	○	○
○	○	○	○	○
You did it!	You did it!	You did it!	You did it!	You did it!

I CAN SAY THE R SOUND!

Say and Dot: Initial IRE Words

Mark the circles below as you practice the IRE sound in words.

Irene	Irish	Ireland	Iron	Iris
◯	◯	◯	◯	◯
◯	◯	◯	◯	◯
◯	◯	◯	◯	◯
◯	◯	◯	◯	◯
◯	◯	◯	◯	◯
◯	◯	◯	◯	◯
◯	◯	◯	◯	◯
You did it!	You did it!	You did it!	You did it!	You did it!

I CAN SAY THE R SOUND!

Say and Dot: Medial IRE Words

Mark the circles below as you practice the IRE sound in words.

Pliers	Firefighter	Tired	Siren	Firewood
○	○	○	○	○
○	○	○	○	○
○	○	○	○	○
○	○	○	○	○
○	○	○	○	○
○	○	○	○	○
○	○	○	○	○
You did it!	You did it!	You did it!	You did it!	You did it!

I CAN SAY THE R SOUND!

Say and Dot: Final IRE Words

Mark the circles below as you practice the IRE sound in words.

Fire	Wire	Tire	Flyer	Vampire
○	○	○	○	○
○	○	○	○	○
○	○	○	○	○
○	○	○	○	○
○	○	○	○	○
○	○	○	○	○
○	○	○	○	○
You did it!	You did it!	You did it!	You did it!	You did it!

I CAN SAY THE R SOUND!

Say and Dot: Initial AIR Words

Mark the circles below as you practice the AIR sound in words.

Arrow	Area	Airplane	Aaron	Air Vent

You did it! You did it! You did it! You did it! You did it!

I CAN SAY THE R SOUND!

Say and Dot: Medial AIR Words

Mark the circles below as you practice the AIR sound in words.

Parrot	Married	Carrot	Wearing	Staring
◯	◯	◯	◯	◯
◯	◯	◯	◯	◯
◯	◯	◯	◯	◯
◯	◯	◯	◯	◯
◯	◯	◯	◯	◯
◯	◯	◯	◯	◯
◯	◯	◯	◯	◯
You did it!	You did it!	You did it!	You did it!	You did it!

I CAN SAY THE R SOUND!

Say and Dot: Final AIR Words

Mark the circles below as you practice the AIR sound in words.

Tear	Pear	There	Bear	Hair
◯	◯	◯	◯	◯
◯	◯	◯	◯	◯
◯	◯	◯	◯	◯
◯	◯	◯	◯	◯
◯	◯	◯	◯	◯
◯	◯	◯	◯	◯
◯	◯	◯	◯	◯
You did it!	You did it!	You did it!	You did it!	You did it!

I CAN SAY THE R SOUND!

Say and Dot: Initial OR Words

Mark the circles below as you practice the OR sound in words.

Orange	Organic	Ornament	Oregon	Orchard

You did it! You did it! You did it! You did it! You did it!

I CAN SAY THE R SOUND!

Say and Dot: Medial OR Words

Mark the circles below as you practice the OR sound in words.

Corn	Bored	Horse	Morning	Fortune
○	○	○	○	○
○	○	○	○	○
○	○	○	○	○
○	○	○	○	○
○	○	○	○	○
○	○	○	○	○
○	○	○	○	○
You did it!	You did it!	You did it!	You did it!	You did it!

150

I CAN SAY THE R SOUND!

Say and Dot: Final OR Words

Mark the circles below as you practice the OR sound in words.

Store 	Pour 	Four 	Door 	Floor 

You did it! (×5)

I CAN SAY THE R SOUND!

Say and Dot: R Blend Words

Mark the circles below as you practice the R blend sound in words.

Tractor	Grow	Grapes	Crab	Presentation
○	○	○	○	○
○	○	○	○	○
○	○	○	○	○
○	○	○	○	○
○	○	○	○	○
○	○	○	○	○
○	○	○	○	○
You did it!	You did it!	You did it!	You did it!	You did it!

I CAN SAY THE R SOUND!

Say and Dot: R Blend Words

Mark the circles below as you practice the R blend sound in words.

Tree	Present	Drum	Dress	Crane
○	○	○	○	○
○	○	○	○	○
○	○	○	○	○
○	○	○	○	○
○	○	○	○	○
○	○	○	○	○
○	○	○	○	○
You did it!	You did it!	You did it!	You did it!	You did it!

I CAN SAY THE R SOUND!

Say and Dot: R Blend Words

Mark the circles below as you practice the R blend sound in words.

Truck	Drill	Trash	Graduate	Grill

You did it!   You did it!   You did it!   You did it!   You did it!

154

I CAN SAY THE R SOUND!

Say and Dot: R Blend Words

Mark the circles below as you practice the R blend sound in words.

Drink	Grapefruit	Bread	Broken	Trail
○	○	○	○	○
○	○	○	○	○
○	○	○	○	○
○	○	○	○	○
○	○	○	○	○
○	○	○	○	○
○	○	○	○	○
You did it!	You did it!	You did it!	You did it!	You did it!

I CAN SAY THE R SOUND!

Say and Dot: High Frequency Initial R Words

Mark the circles below as you practice the R sound.

REST	◯	◯	◯	◯	◯	You did it!
RAN	◯	◯	◯	◯	◯	You did it!
ROUND	◯	◯	◯	◯	◯	You did it!
RULE	◯	◯	◯	◯	◯	You did it!
READY	◯	◯	◯	◯	◯	You did it!
REGION	◯	◯	◯	◯	◯	You did it!
RETURN	◯	◯	◯	◯	◯	You did it!
RAIN	◯	◯	◯	◯	◯	You did it!
WRITTEN	◯	◯	◯	◯	◯	You did it!
REASON	◯	◯	◯	◯	◯	You did it!

I CAN SAY THE R SOUND!

Say and Dot: High Frequency Initial R Words

Mark the circles below as you practice the R sound.

RACE	○	○	○	○	○	You did it!
RECORD	○	○	○	○	○	You did it!
ROOT	○	○	○	○	○	You did it!
RAISED	○	○	○	○	○	You did it!
RESULT	○	○	○	○	○	You did it!
RIDE	○	○	○	○	○	You did it!
ROLLED	○	○	○	○	○	You did it!
REMAIN	○	○	○	○	○	You did it!
ROW	○	○	○	○	○	You did it!
WROTE	○	○	○	○	○	You did it!

I CAN SAY THE R SOUND!

Say and Dot: High Frequency Initial R Words

Mark the circles below as you practice the R sound.

REPORT	○	○	○	○	○	You did it!
RISE	○	○	○	○	○	You did it!
RECEIVED	○	○	○	○	○	You did it!
RING	○	○	○	○	○	You did it!
RATHER	○	○	○	○	○	You did it!
RICH	○	○	○	○	○	You did it!
RYTHM	○	○	○	○	○	You did it!
RADIO	○	○	○	○	○	You did it!
REPEATED	○	○	○	○	○	You did it!
ROPE	○	○	○	○	○	You did it!

I CAN SAY THE R SOUND!

Say and Dot: High Frequency Initial R Blend Words

Mark the circles below as you practice the R sound.

FROM	◯	◯	◯	◯	◯	You did it!
GREAT	◯	◯	◯	◯	◯	You did it!
THROUGH	◯	◯	◯	◯	◯	You did it!
THREE	◯	◯	◯	◯	◯	You did it!
TRY	◯	◯	◯	◯	◯	You did it!
TREE	◯	◯	◯	◯	◯	You did it!
GROUP	◯	◯	◯	◯	◯	You did it!
GROW	◯	◯	◯	◯	◯	You did it!
PROBLEM	◯	◯	◯	◯	◯	You did it!
FRIENDS	◯	◯	◯	◯	◯	You did it!

I CAN SAY THE R SOUND!

Say and Dot: High Frequency Initial R Blend Words

Mark the circles below as you practice the R sound.

PRODUCTS	◯	◯	◯	◯	◯	You did it!
TRUE	◯	◯	◯	◯	◯	You did it!
DRAW	◯	◯	◯	◯	◯	You did it!
CRIED	◯	◯	◯	◯	◯	You did it!
GROUND	◯	◯	◯	◯	◯	You did it!
TRAVEL	◯	◯	◯	◯	◯	You did it!
FRONT	◯	◯	◯	◯	◯	You did it!
PRODUCE	◯	◯	◯	◯	◯	You did it!
GREEN	◯	◯	◯	◯	◯	You did it!
BROUGHT	◯	◯	◯	◯	◯	You did it!

I CAN SAY THE R SOUND!

Say and Dot: High Frequency Initial R Blend Words

Mark the circles below as you practice the R sound.

BRING ○ ○ ○ ○ ○ You did it!

DRY ○ ○ ○ ○ ○ You did it!

TRAIN ○ ○ ○ ○ ○ You did it!

DROP ○ ○ ○ ○ ○ You did it!

PROBABLY ○ ○ ○ ○ ○ You did it!

PRESENT ○ ○ ○ ○ ○ You did it!

GRASS ○ ○ ○ ○ ○ You did it!

DRIVE ○ ○ ○ ○ ○ You did it!

CROSS ○ ○ ○ ○ ○ You did it!

PHRASE ○ ○ ○ ○ ○ You did it!

I CAN SAY THE R SOUND!

Say and Dot: High Frequency Initial R Blend Words

Mark the circles below as you practice the R sound.

FREE ○ ○ ○ ○ ○ *You did it!*

BRIGHT ○ ○ ○ ○ ○ *You did it!*

BROKEN ○ ○ ○ ○ ○ *You did it!*

FRACTION ○ ○ ○ ○ ○ *You did it!*

TRIP ○ ○ ○ ○ ○ *You did it!*

FRENCH ○ ○ ○ ○ ○ *You did it!*

DRESS ○ ○ ○ ○ ○ *You did it!*

GREW ○ ○ ○ ○ ○ *You did it!*

PRESIDENT ○ ○ ○ ○ ○ *You did it!*

BROWN ○ ○ ○ ○ ○ *You did it!*

I CAN SAY THE R SOUND!

Say and Dot: High Frequency Initial R Blend Words

Mark the circles below as you practice the R sound.

TROUBLE	◯ ◯ ◯ ◯ ◯	You did it!
DRAWING	◯ ◯ ◯ ◯ ◯	You did it!
PRACTICE	◯ ◯ ◯ ◯ ◯	You did it!
BREAK	◯ ◯ ◯ ◯ ◯	You did it!
CROPS	◯ ◯ ◯ ◯ ◯	You did it!
PROVIDE	◯ ◯ ◯ ◯ ◯	You did it!
TRADE	◯ ◯ ◯ ◯ ◯	You did it!
CROWD	◯ ◯ ◯ ◯ ◯	You did it!
BRANCHES	◯ ◯ ◯ ◯ ◯	You did it!
FRUIT	◯ ◯ ◯ ◯ ◯	You did it!

I CAN SAY THE R SOUND!

Say and Dot: High Frequency Initial R Blend Words

Mark the circles below as you practice the R sound.

PROCESS ○ ○ ○ ○ ○ *You did it!*

PROPERTY ○ ○ ○ ○ ○ *You did it!*

TRUCK ○ ○ ○ ○ ○ *You did it!*

PRINTED ○ ○ ○ ○ ○ *You did it!*

TRIANGLE ○ ○ ○ ○ ○ *You did it!*

FRANCE ○ ○ ○ ○ ○ *You did it!*

GREEK ○ ○ ○ ○ ○ *You did it!*

CREATE ○ ○ ○ ○ ○ *You did it!*

BRITISH ○ ○ ○ ○ ○ *You did it!*

TRACK ○ ○ ○ ○ ○ *You did it!*

I CAN SAY THE R SOUND!

Say and Dot: High Frequency Medial R Blend Words

Mark the circles below as you practice the R sound.

ACROSS ○ ○ ○ ○ ○ *You did it!*

HUNDRED ○ ○ ○ ○ ○ *You did it!*

PARAGRAPH ○ ○ ○ ○ ○ *You did it!*

REPRESENT ○ ○ ○ ○ ○ *You did it!*

DESCRIBE ○ ○ ○ ○ ○ *You did it!*

AFRICA ○ ○ ○ ○ ○ *You did it!*

EXPRESS ○ ○ ○ ○ ○ *You did it!*

CONTROL ○ ○ ○ ○ ○ *You did it!*

INCREASE ○ ○ ○ ○ ○ *You did it!*

ELECTRIC ○ ○ ○ ○ ○ *You did it!*

I CAN SAY THE R SOUND!

Say and Dot: High Frequency Medial ER Words

Mark the circles below as you practice the R sound.

WORD	○	○	○	○	○	You did it!
FIRST	○	○	○	○	○	You did it!
WORK	○	○	○	○	○	You did it!
TURN	○	○	○	○	○	You did it!
DIFFERENT	○	○	○	○	○	You did it!
LEARN	○	○	○	○	○	You did it!
EARTH	○	○	○	○	○	You did it!
BIRDS	○	○	○	○	○	You did it!
HEARD	○	○	○	○	○	You did it!
HOURS	○	○	○	○	○	You did it!

I CAN SAY THE R SOUND!

Say and Dot: High Frequency Medial ER Words

Mark the circles below as you practice the R sound.

COVERED ○ ○ ○ ○ ○ *You did it!*

PATTERN ○ ○ ○ ○ ○ *You did it!*

CERTAIN ○ ○ ○ ○ ○ *You did it!*

PERSON ○ ○ ○ ○ ○ *You did it!*

VERB ○ ○ ○ ○ ○ *You did it!*

SURFACE ○ ○ ○ ○ ○ *You did it!*

CIRCLE ○ ○ ○ ○ ○ *You did it!*

PERHAPS ○ ○ ○ ○ ○ *You did it!*

ENERGY ○ ○ ○ ○ ○ *You did it!*

RETURN ○ ○ ○ ○ ○ *You did it!*

I CAN SAY THE R SOUND!

Say and Dot: High Frequency Medial ER Words

Mark the circles below as you practice the R sound.

MEMBERS ○ ○ ○ ○ ○ You did it!

EXERCISE ○ ○ ○ ○ ○ You did it!

INTEREST ○ ○ ○ ○ ○ You did it!

THIRD ○ ○ ○ ○ ○ You did it!

FLOWERS ○ ○ ○ ○ ○ You did it!

CENTURY ○ ○ ○ ○ ○ You did it!

BURNING ○ ○ ○ ○ ○ You did it!

SERVE ○ ○ ○ ○ ○ You did it!

DESERT ○ ○ ○ ○ ○ You did it!

MODERN ○ ○ ○ ○ ○ You did it!

I CAN SAY THE R SOUND!

Say and Dot: High Frequency Medial ER Words

Mark the circles below as you practice the R sound.

DOLLARS	○ ○ ○ ○ ○	You did it!
OBSERVE	○ ○ ○ ○ ○	You did it!
PROPERTY	○ ○ ○ ○ ○	You did it!
TERMS	○ ○ ○ ○ ○	You did it!
CURRENT	○ ○ ○ ○ ○	You did it!
SOUTHERN	○ ○ ○ ○ ○	You did it!
WESTERN	○ ○ ○ ○ ○	You did it!
CHURCH	○ ○ ○ ○ ○	You did it!
FORWARD	○ ○ ○ ○ ○	You did it!
DETERMINE	○ ○ ○ ○ ○	You did it!

I CAN SAY THE R SOUND!

Say and Dot: High Frequency Final ER Words

Mark the circles below as you practice the R sound.

WERE	◯ ◯ ◯ ◯ ◯	You did it!
OTHER	◯ ◯ ◯ ◯ ◯	You did it!
HER	◯ ◯ ◯ ◯ ◯	You did it!
NUMBER	◯ ◯ ◯ ◯ ◯	You did it!
WATER	◯ ◯ ◯ ◯ ◯	You did it!
OVER	◯ ◯ ◯ ◯ ◯	You did it!
AFTER	◯ ◯ ◯ ◯ ◯	You did it!
ANOTHER	◯ ◯ ◯ ◯ ◯	You did it!
PICTURE	◯ ◯ ◯ ◯ ◯	You did it!
LETTER	◯ ◯ ◯ ◯ ◯	You did it!

I CAN SAY THE R SOUND!

Say and Dot: High Frequency Final ER Words

Mark the circles below as you practice the R sound.

MOTHER	◯	◯	◯	◯	◯	You did it!
ANSWER	◯	◯	◯	◯	◯	You did it!
FATHER	◯	◯	◯	◯	◯	You did it!
NEVER	◯	◯	◯	◯	◯	You did it!
UNDER	◯	◯	◯	◯	◯	You did it!
PAPER	◯	◯	◯	◯	◯	You did it!
TOGETHER	◯	◯	◯	◯	◯	You did it!
RIVER	◯	◯	◯	◯	◯	You did it!
COLOR	◯	◯	◯	◯	◯	You did it!
EVER	◯	◯	◯	◯	◯	You did it!

171

I CAN SAY THE R SOUND!

Say and Dot: High Frequency Final ER Words

Mark the circles below as you practice the R sound.

ORDER ○ ○ ○ ○ ○ *You did it!*

BETTER ○ ○ ○ ○ ○ *You did it!*

HOWEVER ○ ○ ○ ○ ○ *You did it!*

MEASURE ○ ○ ○ ○ ○ *You did it!*

FIGURE ○ ○ ○ ○ ○ *You did it!*

POWER ○ ○ ○ ○ ○ *You did it!*

MATTER ○ ○ ○ ○ ○ *You did it!*

CENTER ○ ○ ○ ○ ○ *You did it!*

SUMMER ○ ○ ○ ○ ○ *You did it!*

WINTER ○ ○ ○ ○ ○ *You did it!*

I CAN SAY THE R SOUND!

Say and Dot: High Frequency Final ER Words

Mark the circles below as you practice the R sound.

BROTHER ○ ○ ○ ○ ○ You did it!

WHETHER ○ ○ ○ ○ ○ You did it!

TEACHER ○ ○ ○ ○ ○ You did it!

EITHER ○ ○ ○ ○ ○ You did it!

WONDER ○ ○ ○ ○ ○ You did it!

DOCTOR ○ ○ ○ ○ ○ You did it!

RATHER ○ ○ ○ ○ ○ You did it!

CONSIDER ○ ○ ○ ○ ○ You did it!

SIR ○ ○ ○ ○ ○ You did it!

ENTIRE ○ ○ ○ ○ ○ You did it!

I CAN SAY THE R SOUND!

Say and Dot: High Frequency RL Words

Mark the circles below as you practice the R sound.

WORLD	GIRL	SEVERAL	NUMERAL	GENERAL
◯	◯	◯	◯	◯
◯	◯	◯	◯	◯
◯	◯	◯	◯	◯
◯	◯	◯	◯	◯
◯	◯	◯	◯	◯
◯	◯	◯	◯	◯
◯	◯	◯	◯	◯
◯	◯	◯	◯	◯
You did it!	You did it!	You did it!	You did it!	You did it!

I CAN SAY THE R SOUND!

Say and Dot: High Frequency Medial OR Words

Mark the circles below as you practice the R sound.

FORM	STORY	IMPORTANT	HORSE	SHORT
◯	◯	◯	◯	◯
◯	◯	◯	◯	◯
◯	◯	◯	◯	◯
◯	◯	◯	◯	◯
◯	◯	◯	◯	◯
◯	◯	◯	◯	◯
◯	◯	◯	◯	◯
◯	◯	◯	◯	◯
You did it!	You did it!	You did it!	You did it!	You did it!

I CAN SAY THE R SOUND!

Say and Dot: High Frequency Medial OR Words

Mark the circles below as you practice the R sound.

TOWARD	MORNING	NORTH	COURSE	FORCE
◯	◯	◯	◯	◯
◯	◯	◯	◯	◯
◯	◯	◯	◯	◯
◯	◯	◯	◯	◯
◯	◯	◯	◯	◯
◯	◯	◯	◯	◯
◯	◯	◯	◯	◯
◯	◯	◯	◯	◯
You did it!	You did it!	You did it!	You did it!	You did it!

I CAN SAY THE R SOUND!

Say and Dot: High Frequency Medial OR Words

Mark the circles below as you practice the R sound.

WARM	FOREST	RECORD	REPORT	BOARD
◯	◯	◯	◯	◯
◯	◯	◯	◯	◯
◯	◯	◯	◯	◯
◯	◯	◯	◯	◯
◯	◯	◯	◯	◯
◯	◯	◯	◯	◯
◯	◯	◯	◯	◯
◯	◯	◯	◯	◯
You did it!	You did it!	You did it!	You did it!	You did it!

I CAN SAY THE R SOUND!

Say and Dot: High Frequency Final OR Words

Mark the circles below as you practice the R sound.

POOR	YOUR	MORE	BEFORE	FOUR
◯	◯	◯	◯	◯
◯	◯	◯	◯	◯
◯	◯	◯	◯	◯
◯	◯	◯	◯	◯
◯	◯	◯	◯	◯
◯	◯	◯	◯	◯
◯	◯	◯	◯	◯
◯	◯	◯	◯	◯
You did it!	You did it!	You did it!	You did it!	You did it!

I CAN SAY THE R SOUND!

Say and Dot: High Frequency Final OR Words

Mark the circles below as you practice the R sound.

DOOR	WAR	STORE	FLOOR	SCORE
○	○	○	○	○
○	○	○	○	○
○	○	○	○	○
○	○	○	○	○
○	○	○	○	○
○	○	○	○	○
○	○	○	○	○
○	○	○	○	○
You did it!	You did it!	You did it!	You did it!	You did it!

I CAN SAY THE R SOUND!

Say and Dot: High Frequency Final EAR Words

Mark the circles below as you practice the R sound.

HERE	NEAR	CLEAR	APPEAR	FEAR
○	○	○	○	○
○	○	○	○	○
○	○	○	○	○
○	○	○	○	○
○	○	○	○	○
○	○	○	○	○
○	○	○	○	○
○	○	○	○	○
You did it!	You did it!	You did it!	You did it!	You did it!

I CAN SAY THE R SOUND!

Say and Dot: RL Words

Mark the circles below as you practice the R sound.

GIRL	PEARL	HURL	CURL	WHIRL
◯	◯	◯	◯	◯
◯	◯	◯	◯	◯
◯	◯	◯	◯	◯
◯	◯	◯	◯	◯
◯	◯	◯	◯	◯
◯	◯	◯	◯	◯
◯	◯	◯	◯	◯
◯	◯	◯	◯	◯
You did it!	You did it!	You did it!	You did it!	You did it!

INITIAL R MATCHING

Listen to the words as they are read aloud. Then, draw a line to match the word to the corresponding picture on the right side of the page. Then, practice saying the word with an accurate R sound.

RICH

RIDE

RIPE

RING

ROCK

RUN

MEDIAL R MATCHING

Listen to the words as they are read aloud. Then, draw a line to match the word to the corresponding picture on the right side of the page. Then, practice saying the word with an accurate R sound.

CARROT

BERRY

PIRATE

PURRING

FURRY

EARRINGS

FINAL R MATCHING

Listen to the words as they are read aloud. Then, draw a line to match the word to the corresponding picture on the right side of the page. Then, practice saying the word with an accurate R sound.

MOTHER

FEATHER

BAKER

LOCKER

DOLLAR

FIRE

R BLENDS MATCHING

Listen to the words as they are read aloud. Then, draw a line to match the word to the corresponding picture on the right side of the page. Then, practice saying the word with an accurate R sound.

DRINK

BROKEN

BREAD

TRAIL

GRILL

GRAPEFRUIT

R BLENDS MATCHING

Listen to the words as they are read aloud. Then, draw a line to match the word to the corresponding picture on the right side of the page. Then, practice saying the word with an accurate R sound.

CRANE

DRESS

DRILL

TRUCK

TRASH

GRADUATE

R BLENDS MATCHING

Listen to the words as they are read aloud. Then, draw a line to match the word to the corresponding picture on the right side of the page. Then, practice saying the word with an accurate R sound.

PRESENT

GRAPES

DRUM

TREE

TRACTOR

CRAB

DRAW AND PRACTICE

Think of 10 things that start with the R sound and draw them in the space below. Then, practice saying each word 10 times.

RRRRRRRR

TIMED ARTICULATION

You will need a timer for this activity. A sand timer is recommended, but other timers may be used. Start your timer and see how many R words you can say correctly before the time runs out. Record the number of words you said on the score sheet, and play again! How many words can you say during one speech therapy session?

INITIAL R

RAN	RANG	RAT
RABBIT	RADISH	RAG
RAP	RED	READY
REST	RING	RICH
RIVER	RIBBON	ROCK
ROBIN	RUN	RAKE
RACE	RAIN	RADIO
REACH	REAL	RIPE
RICE	ROW	ROLL
ROAD	ROOM	ROACH

TIMED ARTICULATION

You will need a timer for this activity. A sand timer is recommended, but other timers may be used. Start your timer and see how many R words you can say correctly before the time runs out. Record the number of words you said on the score sheet, and play again! How many words can you say during one speech therapy session?

MEDIAL R

AROUND	VERY	CARRY
FAIRY	GARDEN	FOREST
STORY	CARROT	ARROW
TOMORROW	PORRIDGE	BEDROOM
ORANGE	TERRIBLE	TERRANCE
MARRIED	HERON	DAIRY
SHARING	PARENT	CURRENT
FURNISH	PURCHASE	BERRY
WEARING	FORTUNE	TORNADO
TOURNAMENT	WORRY	SCARY

TIMED ARTICULATION

You will need a timer for this activity. A sand timer is recommended, but other timers may be used. Start your timer and see how many R words you can say correctly before the time runs out. Record the number of words you said on the score sheet, and play again! How many words can you say during one speech therapy session?

FINAL R

FOUR	BEAR	DEER
EAR	TEAR	PEAR
JAR	ALLIGATOR	DOCTOR
FEATHER	DOLLAR	MOTHER
HAMMER	LADDER	CAR
CHAIR	DOOR	TIRE
HAIR	BEAVER	LETTER
DINOSAUR	FLOWER	FATHER
BAKER	WONDER	FEAR
TIGER	TEACHER	FINGER

TIMED ARTICULATION

You will need a timer for this activity. A sand timer is recommended, but other timers may be used. Start your timer and see how many R words you can say correctly before the time runs out. Record the number of words you said on the score sheet, and play again! How many words can you say during one speech therapy session?

ER WORDS

EARLY	EARTH	EARTHWORM
EARL	EARNEST	URBAN
CURSIVE	MIXTURE	SISTER
SKIRT	FIRST	HEARD
TURN	LEARN	MOTHER
FERN	WHISPER	NEVER
SPIDER	BUTTER	PURSE
HURT	STIR	DIRT
GERMS	TURKEY	TEACHER
FATHER	CREATURE	COVER

TIMED ARTICULATION

You will need a timer for this activity. A sand timer is recommended, but other timers may be used. Start your timer and see how many R words you can say correctly before the time runs out. Record the number of words you said on the score sheet, and play again! How many words can you say during one speech therapy session?

AR WORDS

ARMY	ARTIST	AARDVARK
ARSON	ART	ARTWORK
ARM	ARTISTIC	CART
START	MARBLE	GUARD
SPARKLE	HEART	YARD
CARD	DART	CAR
FAR	TAR	BAR
ALARM	MARKET	YARN
FARM	HARP	TARP
GARNISH	STAR	TART

TIMED ARTICULATION

You will need a timer for this activity. A sand timer is recommended, but other timers may be used. Start your timer and see how many R words you can say correctly before the time runs out. Record the number of words you said on the score sheet, and play again! How many words can you say during one speech therapy session?

EAR WORDS

FEAR	STEER	IRRITATED
YEAR	HERO	JEER
HEAR	NEAR	PIER
HEARING	SPEAR	BEARD
CHEER	GEAR	DISAPPEAR
PIONEER	SOUVENIR	CASHIER
PERIOD	CHANDELIER	CHEERING
CEREAL	PYRAMID	WEIRD
CAFETERIA	EAR	EARWIG
EARRING	EERIE	PIERCING

TIMED ARTICULATION

You will need a timer for this activity. A sand timer is recommended, but other timers may be used. Start your timer and see how many R words you can say correctly before the time runs out. Record the number of words you said on the score sheet, and play again! How many words can you say during one speech therapy session?

IRE WORDS

CHOIR	FLIER	PLIERS
UMPIRE	DRYER	TIRED
FIRE	CAMPFIRE	IRELAND
IRENE	WIRING	DIRE
LIAR	BUYER	HIRE
WIRE	EMPIRE	BRIAR
ADMIRE	VAMPIRE	SAPPHIRE
TIRE	IRONING	FIREMAN
SIRE	IRON	IRISH
IRAN	DESIRE	EXPIRE

TIMED ARTICULATION

You will need a timer for this activity. A sand timer is recommended, but other timers may be used. Start your timer and see how many R words you can say correctly before the time runs out. Record the number of words you said on the score sheet, and play again! How many words can you say during one speech therapy session?

AIR WORDS

PARENTS	SHERIFF	AIRPLANE
AIR	ARROW	ARROGANT
AIRFORCE	WHERE	BAREFOOT
MARRIED	SQUARE	LAIR
MARE	DARE	CARE
STARE	SHARE	FAIR
STEREO	MARATHON	ASPARAGUS
PARROT	CHERRY	DAIRY
PARACHUTE	ERIN	HAIRY
BURY	CARING	STARING

TIMED ARTICULATION

You will need a timer for this activity. A sand timer is recommended, but other timers may be used. Start your timer and see how many R words you can say correctly before the time runs out. Record the number of words you said on the score sheet, and play again! How many words can you say during one speech therapy session?

OR WORDS

BOARD	SHORTS	SHORE
STORY	POUR	SPORT
SWORD	SHORT	FORT
POPCORN	STORM	THORN
ORGAN	MORNING	HORSESHOE
TORNADO	STORE	FLOOR
ORNATE	MORE	SCORE
NORTH	PORT	CHORE
ORANGE	FOREST	ORVILLE
ORCHID	ORIGINAL	ORNAMENT

TIMED ARTICULATION

You will need a timer for this activity. A sand timer is recommended, but other timers may be used. Start your timer and see how many R words you can say correctly before the time runs out. Record the number of words you said on the score sheet, and play again! How many words can you say during one speech therapy session?

R BLENDS

BRING	BRICK	CRY
CROWD	DRAW	DRESS
FRIEND	FROG	GROW
GRAY	PRESENT	PRINCE
BRIGHT	BREAD	BREAKFAST
CROWN	CRIB	CRAB
DROP	DREAM	FRESH
FRUIT	FREEZE	FRIGHTEN
GRAPE	GREEN	GRANDMA
GRACE	PRIZE	PRETTY

TIMED ARTICULATION

SCORE SHEET

NAME: _____

DATE: _____

	NUMBER OF WORDS PRACTICED
TRIAL 1	
TRIAL 2	
TRIAL 3	
TRIAL 4	
TRIAL 5	
TOTAL	

	NUMBER OF WORDS PRACTICED
TRIAL 1	
TRIAL 2	
TRIAL 3	
TRIAL 4	
TRIAL 5	
TOTAL	

	NUMBER OF WORDS PRACTICED
TRIAL 1	
TRIAL 2	
TRIAL 3	
TRIAL 4	
TRIAL 5	
TOTAL	

	NUMBER OF WORDS PRACTICED
TRIAL 1	
TRIAL 2	
TRIAL 3	
TRIAL 4	
TRIAL 5	
TOTAL	

SPIN IT, SAY IT, COLOR IT

Put a paperclip in the middle of the spinner circle. Then, stick the tip of a pencil through one end of the paperclip to form a "spinner." Spin the paperclip. Whatever number it lands on is how many times you must practice one of the R words pictured on the page. Select the word you want to practice, say it the correct number of times, and then color the picture. Do this until all of the pictures are colored.

INITIAL R

RAFT

RAIN

RIP

ROCKET

ROBIN

RIBBON

RAT

RECYCLE

RUNWAY

RADIO

SPIN IT, SAY IT, COLOR IT

Put a paperclip in the middle of the spinner circle. Then, stick the tip of a pencil through one end of the paperclip to form a "spinner." Spin the paperclip. Whatever number it lands on is how many times you must practice one of the R words pictured on the page. Select the word you want to practice, say it the correct number of times, and then color the picture. Do this until all of the pictures are colored.

INITIAL R

10

5   5

10

ROBOT

RESEARCH

A

ROOF

ROCKING HORSE

RING

WRITE

ROBE

ROLL

ROWBOAT

RAPPEL

SPIN IT, SAY IT, COLOR IT

Put a paperclip in the middle of the spinner circle. Then, stick the tip of a pencil through one end of the paperclip to form a "spinner." Spin the paperclip. Whatever number it lands on is how many times you must practice one of the R words pictured on the page. Select the word you want to practice, say it the correct number of times, and then color the picture. Do this until all of the pictures are colored.

MEDIAL R

CAMERA

PARAKEET

EXERCISE

HEART

CIRCUS TENT

LIZARD

CERTIFICATE

SKIRT

BARN

GIRAFFE

SPIN IT, SAY IT, COLOR IT

Put a paperclip in the middle of the spinner circle. Then, stick the tip of a pencil through one end of the paperclip to form a "spinner." Spin the paperclip. Whatever number it lands on is how many times you must practice one of the R words pictured on the page. Select the word you want to practice, say it the correct number of times, and then color the picture. Do this until all of the pictures are colored.

MEDIAL R

ENERGY

MARSHMALLOW

ALARM

SHIRT

HYDRANT

EARRINGS

TURTLE

TURKEY

SIREN

PAPERCLIP

SPIN IT, SAY IT, COLOR IT

Put a paperclip in the middle of the spinner circle. Then, stick the tip of a pencil through one end of the paperclip to form a "spinner." Spin the paperclip. Whatever number it lands on is how many times you must practice one of the R words pictured on the page. Select the word you want to practice, say it the correct number of times, and then color the picture. Do this until all of the pictures are colored.

FINAL R

DOOR

FIRE

MOTHER

GUITAR

TRAILER

PRESENTER

OFFICER

HAMMER

SHOP

HAMSTER

STORE

SPIN IT, SAY IT, COLOR IT

Put a paperclip in the middle of the spinner circle. Then, stick the tip of a pencil through one end of the paperclip to form a "spinner." Spin the paperclip. Whatever number it lands on is how many times you must practice one of the R words pictured on the page. Select the word you want to practice, say it the correct number of times, and then color the picture. Do this until all of the pictures are colored.

FINAL R

NEWSPAPER

POUR

CHAIR

DEER

THEATER

DOCTOR

HEAR

HIKER

JUGGLER

TOWER

SPIN IT, SAY IT, COLOR IT

Put a paperclip in the middle of the spinner circle. Then, stick the tip of a pencil through one end of the paperclip to form a "spinner." Spin the paperclip. Whatever number it lands on is how many times you must practice one of the R words pictured on the page. Select the word you want to practice, say it the correct number of times, and then color the picture. Do this until all of the pictures are colored.

R BLENDS

CRAB

PRESENTATION

CRANE

TRACTOR

DRESS

GROW

TREE

PRESENT

GRAPES

DRUM

SPIN IT, SAY IT, COLOR IT

Put a paperclip in the middle of the spinner circle. Then, stick the tip of a pencil through one end of the paperclip to form a "spinner." Spin the paperclip. Whatever number it lands on is how many times you must practice one of the R words pictured on the page. Select the word you want to practice, say it the correct number of times, and then color the picture. Do this until all of the pictures are colored.

R BLENDS

GRADUATE

GRILL

TRASH

BREAD

DRINK

DRILL

GRAPEFRUIT

TRUCK

TRAIL

BROKEN

NONSENSE WORD FUN

Make up some nonsense words that have the R sound in them! Write your words in the spaces below. Then, practice your words 5 times each. Check a box each time you practice.

I CAN SAY THE R SOUND!

Play tic-tac-toe, but before you take your turn, say the R-word in the square you plan to mark.

ARTICULATION TIC-TAC-TOE!

INITIAL R

ROWBOAT	ROBIN	WRITE
ROBE	RING	ROLL
ROBOT	RAFT	RECYCLE

INITIAL R

RAIN	ROCKET	ROAST
RADIO	RUNWAY	RAPPEL
RUN	RAIL	RAT

MEDIAL R

TURKEY	SHIRT	SKIRT
PAPERCLIP	EARRINGS	TURTLE
 ALARM CLOCK	ENERGY	SIREN

FINAL R

POUR	HAMSTER	CHAIR
HAMMER	SOCCER	NEWSPAPER
 DOOR	GUITAR	DOCTOR

I CAN SAY THE R SOUND!

Play tic-tac-toe, but before you take your turn, say the R-word in the square you plan to mark.

ARTICULATION TIC-TAC-TOE!

INITIAL R

race	rest	room
ride	ring	road
round	rock	rat

INITIAL R

rain	rice	real
roll	rhyme	ran
rope	rule	ram

INITIAL R

rug	recess	wrap
write	wrist	rake
read	rip	roach

INITIAL R

reason	robot	remind
reach	radio	raisin
ranch	repeat	really

I CAN SAY THE R SOUND!

Play tic-tac-toe, but before you take your turn, say the R-word in the square you plan to mark.

ARTICULATION TIC-TAC-TOE!

MEDIAL AR

barn	cart	shark
start	tarp	large
bark	yard	dark

MEDIAL ER

burn	purse	turn
dirt	learn	girl
turkey	first	skirt

MEDIAL AIR

parent	fairy	staring
married	stereo	cherry
parrot	carrot	hairy

MEDIAL OR

corn	fort	torn
shorts	story	storm
morning	forest	bored

I CAN SAY THE R SOUND!

Play tic-tac-toe, but before you take your turn, say the R-word in the square you plan to mark.

ARTICULATION TIC-TAC-TOE!

FINAL VOCALIC AR

jar	far	star
bar	scar	ajar
tar	car	guitar

FINAL VOCALIC ER

her	stir	teacher
were	fur	feather
blur	better	monster

FINAL VOCALIC AIR

pear	stare	bear
where	there	tear
scare	fair	chair

FINAL VOCALIC OR

pour	score	more
four	store	tore
wore	chore	floor

I CAN SAY THE R SOUND!

Play tic-tac-toe, but before you take your turn, say the R-word in the square you plan to mark.

ARTICULATION TIC-TAC-TOE!

VOCALIC IRE

iron	Irish	irene
tired	pliers	tires
fire	hire	vampire

VOCALIC EAR

ear	earring	irritated
weird	hero	cereal
fear	near	steer

R-BLENDS

brown	bright	Friday
crown	gray	price
drive	grow	treat

R-BLENDS

frown	tree	cry
pretty	green	bring
gross	through	fright

R CLUES: CUT AND PASTE | INITIAL R

Cut out the pictures at the bottom of the page. Read the clues and then select the picture that the clues are describing. Glue the picture in the corresponding box and then practice the R word 10 times.

I am colorful and can be found in the sky. Some legends say that you'll find a pot of gold at the end of my colorful stripes. What am I? →

I am a small furry animal. I have long ears. I hop from place to place and like to eat carrots. What am I? →

I fall from the sky and water the plants on the ground. You might need an umbrella if you don't want me to get you wet! What am I? →

I am hard and black. I have lines painted on my surface. Cars drive on me as they move through the city. What am I? →

Race

Rain

Road

Rabbit

Rainbow

R CLUES: CUT AND PASTE | INITIAL R

Cut out the pictures at the bottom of the page. Read the clues and then select the picture that the clues are describing. Glue the picture in the corresponding box and then practice the R word 10 times.

Cowboys use me at rodeos. I can be tied into knots. I am very useful. What am I?

→

I am a small animal with fur. I have a long hairless tail. I can be a pet or I can live in the wild. What am I?

→

I am made of metal. I have buttons and can do many different things. I make beeping noises. What am I?

→

I am part of a house. I keep the people in the house from getting wet when it rains. I am made of shingles. What am I?

→

Robot

Roof

Rat

Rope

Razor

R CLUES: CUT AND PASTE | ER WORDS

Cut out the pictures at the bottom of the page. Read the clues and then select the picture that the clues are describing. Glue the picture in the corresponding box and then practice the R word 10 times.

I am loud and powerful. When your grass is long, you use me to cut it shorter. What am I? →

I am soft. I cover the body of animals such as dogs, cats, and rabbits. I can be many different colors such as brown, black, or white. What am I? →

I am a sport. When I'm played, people kick a black and white ball around a field. What am I? →

I am light and soft. You can find me on birds. Sometimes, I am also found inside pillows. What am I? →

Fur

Lawn Mower

Helicopter

Soccer

Feather

R CLUES: CUT AND PASTE | AR WORDS

Cut out the pictures at the bottom of the page. Read the clues and then select the picture that the clues are describing. Glue the picture in the corresponding box and then practice the R word 10 times.

I am found on a farm. I am a large building. Animals live in me. I can also be used to store hay and other supplies. What am I? →

I am a container. I can hold drinks such as your milk at school. What am I? →

I am metal or plastic. You find me in stores. You push me around while you shop and put things in me. What am I? →

I'm a strange creature. I live in outer space. I ride in a spaceship. What am I? →

Barn

Tart

Carton

Martian

Cart

R CLUES: CUT AND PASTE | AR WORDS

Cut out the pictures at the bottom of the page. Read the clues and then select the picture that the clues are describing. Glue the picture in the corresponding box and then practice the R word 10 times.

I twinkle bright in the night sky. There are many of me shining above. What am I? →

I am a container for storing foods such as jam or mayonnaise. I have a lid that screws on tight. What am I? →

I am a common vehicle. I take people places. I have four wheels and a steering wheel. What am I? →

I am sticky and gooey. I'm a dark brown or black liquid. I can be derived from coal or wood. What am I? →

Star

Car

Jar

Tar

Candy bar

R CLUES: CUT AND PASTE

EAR WORDS

Cut out the pictures at the bottom of the page. Read the clues and then select the picture that the clues are describing. Glue the picture in the corresponding box and then practice the R word 10 times.

I do wonderful things and help other people. I wear a cape. I can have super powers. What am I?

→

I am a common breakfast food. You put me in a bowl and pour milk on top. You eat me with a spoon. What am I?

→

I am hair that grows on a man's face. I grow on his chin and cheeks. What am I?

→

I am a place where students eat lunch at school. Food is served here. I have tables and chairs. What am I?

→

Piercing

Hero

Cafeteria

Cereal

Beard

225

R CLUES: CUT AND PASTE | IRE WORDS

Cut out the pictures at the bottom of the page. Read the clues and then select the picture that the clues are describing. Glue the picture in the corresponding box and then practice the R word 10 times.

I am a piece of paper that has important information on it. I can be hung on bulletin boards or handed out to people. What am I?

→

I am very hot. When people go camping, they use me for warmth or to help cook food. You can also find me burning candles. What am I?

→

I am a scary creature. I have sharp fangs. I wear a cape. I am seen during Halloween. What am I?

→

I am seen on vehicles. I am round. I am made of rubber. I help vehicles roll where they need to go. What am I?

→

 Wire

 Tire

 Fire

 Vampire

 Flyer

R CLUES: CUT AND PASTE | AIR WORDS

Cut out the pictures at the bottom of the page. Read the clues and then select the picture that the clues are describing. Glue the picture in the corresponding box and then practice the R word 10 times.

I am a small red fruit. I can be eaten plain or blended with other fruits to make a smoothie. I am sweet and juicy. What am I? →

I am a crunchy orange vegetable. I grow underground. Rabbits love to eat me. What am I? →

I have a child. I teach my child how to do things, cook meals for them, and love spending time with them. What am I? →

I have a handle and bristles. I am usually stored in the bathroom. I am can make your hair look nice and neat. What am I? →

Berry

Marry

Parent

Hairbrush

Carrot

R CLUES: CUT AND PASTE | AIR WORDS

Cut out the pictures at the bottom of the page. Read the clues and then select the picture that the clues are describing. Glue the picture in the corresponding box and then practice the R word 10 times.

I am a small fruit. I am red and round. I have a long stem. I have a hard pit inside of me. What am I?

→

I can show you which direction to go. I point to things with my triangular shaped top. What am I?

→

I am something you can ride in. I can be pulled by horses. I have big wheels. I am fancy and often associated with royalty. What am I?

→

I am a small furry rodent. I have a long body and a cute face with whiskers. I am often kept as a pet. What am I?

→

Cherry

Arrow

Parrot

Ferret

Carriage

R CLUES: CUT AND PASTE

OR WORDS

Cut out the pictures at the bottom of the page. Read the clues and then select the picture that the clues are describing. Glue the picture in the corresponding box and then practice the R word 10 times.

I'm a citrus fruit. I grow in warm climates such as Florida. I have a thick peel. I am often used to make juice.

I am round and fragile. You hang me on trees during the holiday season. I come in many colors and styles. What am I?

I am a state in the United States of America. I am in the Northwest. My capital is Salem. What am I?

I am a collection of trees. The trees grow fruit. People can come and pick the fruit. What am I?

Ornament

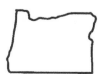

Oregon

Organic

Orchard

Orange

RACE TO THE FINISH LINE: DICE GAME

INITIAL

Each player will have their own sheet and take turns rolling the dice. Roll the dice and color in one race car under the number that you roll. Practice the R word on your car 10 times. Whoever fills up a row and makes it to the finish line first wins!

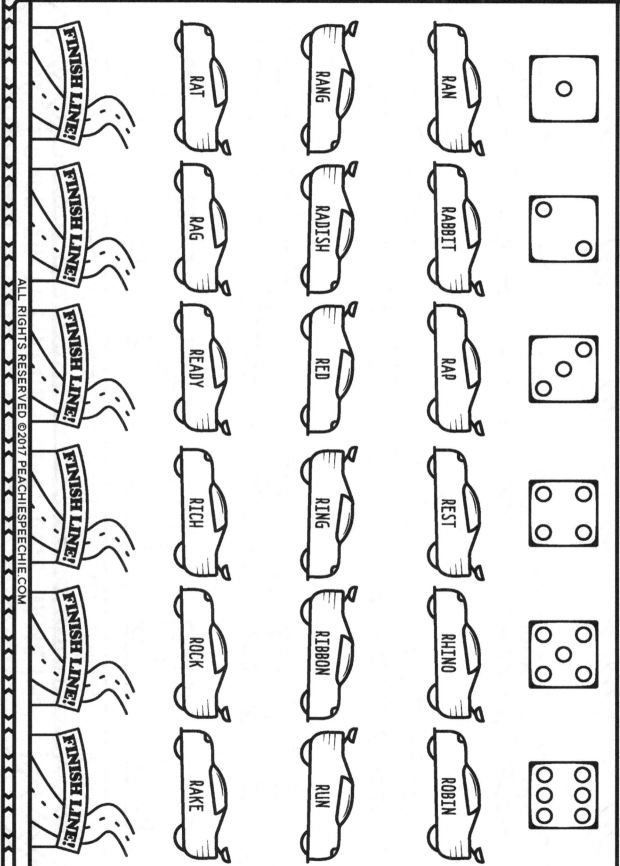

•	RAN	RABBIT	RAP	REST	RHINO	ROBIN	FINISH LINE!
RANG	RADISH	RED	RING	RIBBON	RUN	FINISH LINE!
RAT	RAG	READY	RICH	ROCK	RAKE	FINISH LINE!

RACE TO THE FINISH LINE: DICE GAME

MEDIAL

Each player will have their own sheet and take turns rolling the dice. Roll the dice and color in one race car under the number that you roll. Practice the R word on your car 10 times. Whoever fills up a row and makes it to the finish line first wins!

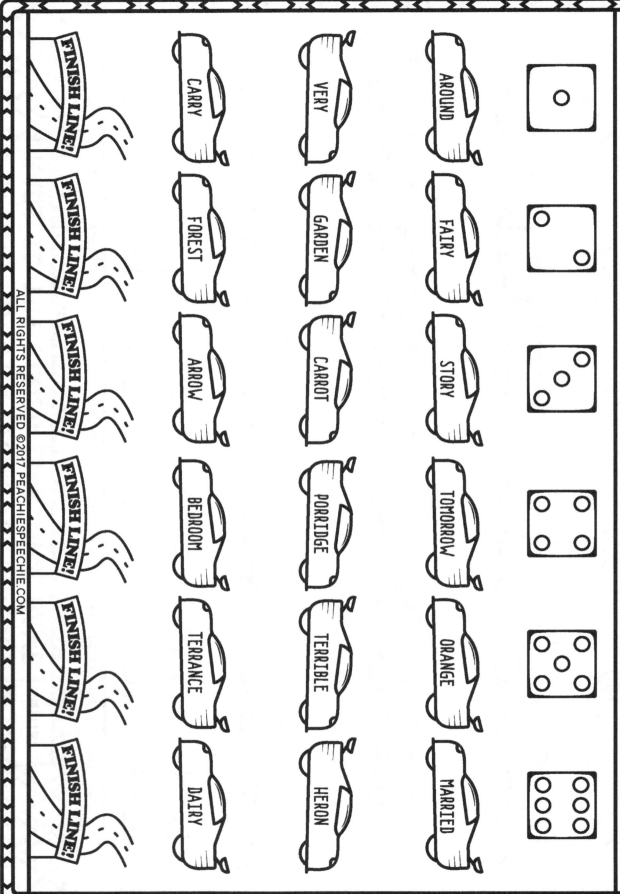

Dice	Car 1	Car 2	Car 3	Finish
⚀	AROUND	VERY	CARRY	FINISH LINE!
⚁	FAIRY	GARDEN	FOREST	FINISH LINE!
⚂	STORY	CARROT	ARROW	FINISH LINE!
⚃	TOMORROW	PORRIDGE	BEDROOM	FINISH LINE!
⚄	ORANGE	TERRIBLE	TERRANCE	FINISH LINE!
⚅	MARRIED	HERON	DAIRY	FINISH LINE!

235

Each player will have their own sheet and take turns rolling the dice. Roll the dice and color in one race car under the number that you roll. Practice the R word on your car 10 times. Whoever fills up a row and makes it to the finish line first wins!

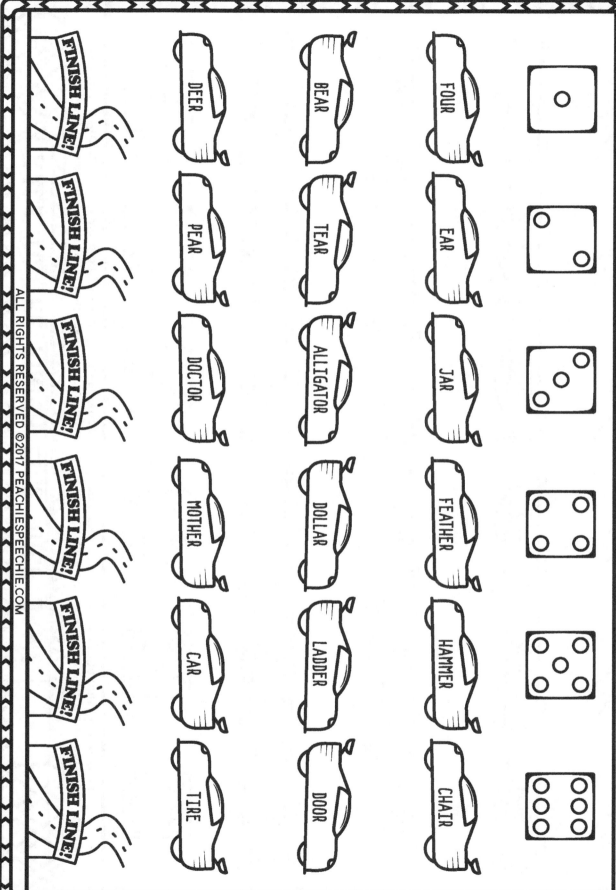

FOUR
EAR
JAR
FEATHER
HAMMER
CHAIR

BEAR
TEAR
ALLIGATOR
DOLLAR
LADDER
DOOR

DEER
PEAR
DOCTOR
MOTHER
CAR
TIRE

FINISH LINE!
FINISH LINE!
FINISH LINE!
FINISH LINE!
FINISH LINE!
FINISH LINE!

RACE TO THE FINISH LINE: DICE GAME

ER

Each player will have their own sheet and take turns rolling the dice. Roll the dice and color in one race car under the number that you roll. Practice the R word on your car 10 times. Whoever fills up a row and makes it to the finish line first wins!

⚀	⚁	⚂	⚃	⚄	⚅	
EARLY	EARL	CURSIVE	SKIRT	TURN	FERN	FINISH LINE!
EARTH	EARNEST	MIXTURE	FIRST	LEARN	WHISPER	FINISH LINE!
WORM	URBAN	SISTER	HEARD	MOTHER	NEVER	FINISH LINE!

237

RACE TO THE FINISH LINE: DICE GAME

AR

Each player will have their own sheet and take turns rolling the dice. Roll the dice and color in one race car under the number that you roll. Practice the R word on your car 10 times. Whoever fills up a row and makes it to the finish line first wins!

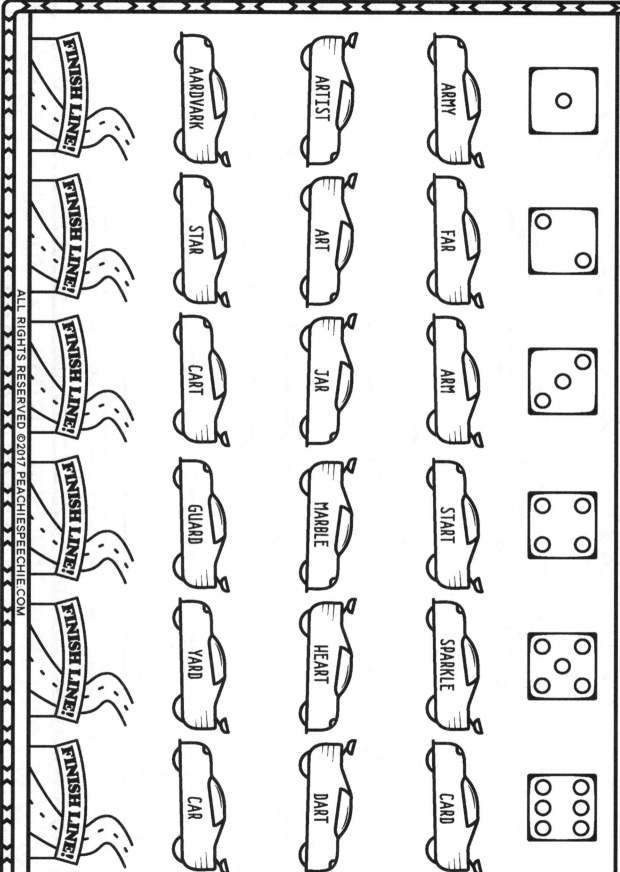

⚀	⚁	⚂	⚃	⚄	⚅
ARMY	FAR	ARM	START	SPARKLE	CARD
ARTIST	ART	JAR	MARBLE	HEART	DART
AARDVARK	STAR	CART	GUARD	YARD	CAR
FINISH LINE!	FINISH LINE!	FINISH LINE!	FINISH LINE!	FINISH LINE!	FINISH LINE!

ALL RIGHTS RESERVED ©2017 PEACHIESPEECHIE.COM

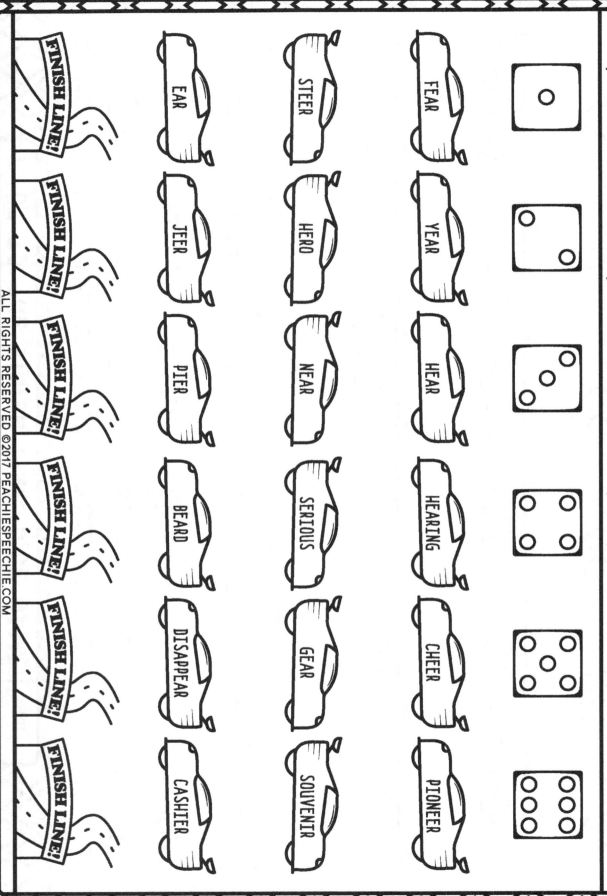

238

RACE TO THE FINISH LINE: DICE GAME

Each player will have their own sheet and take turns rolling the dice. Roll the dice and color in one race car under the number that you roll. Practice the R word on your car 10 times. Whoever fills up a row and makes it to the finish line first wins!

EAR

FEAR	YEAR	HEAR	HEARING	CHEER	PIONEER
STEER	HERO	NEAR	SERIOUS	GEAR	SOUVENIR
EAR	JEER	PIER	BEARD	DISAPPEAR	CASHIER

FINISH LINE!

RACE TO THE FINISH LINE: DICE GAME

IRE

Each player will have their own sheet and take turns rolling the dice. Roll the dice and color in one race car under the number that you roll. Practice the R word on your car 10 times. Whoever fills up a row and makes it to the finish line first wins!

•	CHOIR	UMPIRE	FIRE	IRENE	LIAR	WIRE
••	FLIER	DRYER	CAMPFIRE	WIRING	BUYER	EMPIRE
•••	PLIERS	TIRED	IRELAND	SIREN	HIRE	BRIAR

FINISH LINE! FINISH LINE! FINISH LINE! FINISH LINE! FINISH LINE! FINISH LINE!

RACE TO THE FINISH LINE: DICE GAME

AIR

Each player will have their own sheet and take turns rolling the dice. Roll the dice and color in one race car under the number that you roll. Practice the R word on your car 10 times. Whoever fills up a row and makes it to the finish line first wins!

⚀	⚁	⚂	⚃	⚄	⚅	
PARENTS	AIR	AIRFORCE	MARRIED	MARE	STARE	FINISH LINE!
SHERIFF	ARROW	WHERE	SQUARE	DARE	SHARE	FINISH LINE!
AIRPLANE	ARROGANT	BAREFOOT	LAIR	CARE	FAIR	FINISH LINE!

RACE TO THE FINISH LINE: DICE GAME

OR

Each player will have their own sheet and take turns rolling the dice. Roll the dice and color in one race car under the number that you roll. Practice the R word on your car 10 times. Whoever fills up a row and makes it to the finish line first wins!

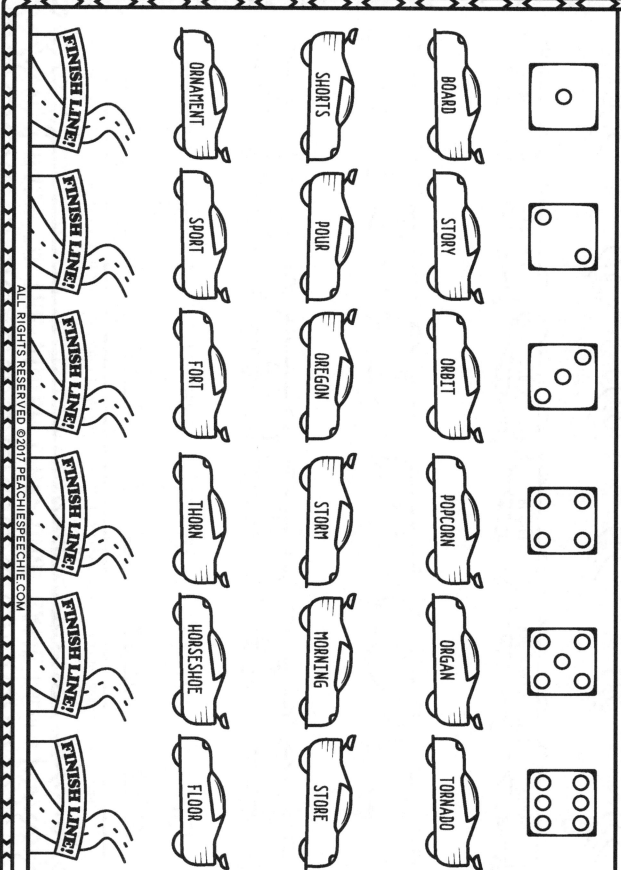

⚀	⚁	⚂	⚃	⚄	⚅
BOARD	STORY	ORBIT	POPCORN	ORGAN	TORNADO
SHORTS	POUR	OREGON	STORM	MORNING	STORE
ORNAMENT	SPORT	FORT	THORN	HORSESHOE	FLOOR
FINISH LINE!	FINISH LINE!	FINISH LINE!	FINISH LINE!	FINISH LINE!	FINISH LINE!

RACE TO THE FINISH LINE: DICE GAME

BLENDS

Each player will have their own sheet and take turns rolling the dice. Roll the dice and color in one race car under the number that you roll. Practice the R word on your car 10 times. Whoever fills up a row and makes it to the finish line first wins!

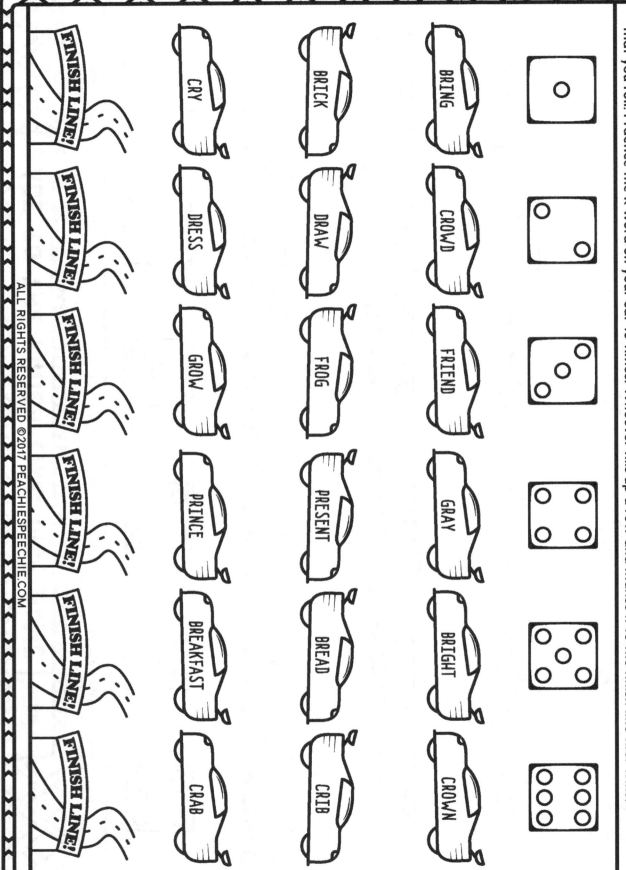

BRING	CROWD	FRIEND	FINISH LINE!
BRICK	DRAW	FROG	FINISH LINE!
CRY	DRESS	GROW	FINISH LINE!
	PRINCE	GRAY	FINISH LINE!
	PRESENT	BRIGHT	FINISH LINE!
	BREAKFAST	BREAD	FINISH LINE!
	CRAB	CRIB	CROWN

UNSCRAMBLE THE R WORDS

The letters below are out of order! Unscramble the letters to make a word that starts with the R sound. Write the word on the line. Then, practice saying the word 5 times. If you need a hint, look at the pictures at the bottom of the page. All of the scrambled words are pictured.

INITIAL R
Level 1

DREA _____

YDAER _____

NIRA _____

ORDIA _____

HICR _____

NDRUO _____

WORD BANK

| ROUND | RAIN | RICH | RADIO | READY | READ |

UNSCRAMBLE THE R WORDS

The letters below are out of order! Unscramble the letters to make an R sound in the middle of the word. Write the word on the line. Then, practice saying the word 5 times. If you need a hint, look at the pictures at the bottom of the page. All of the scrambled words are pictured.

MEDIAL R
Level 1

KADR _____

NAREL _____

YROST _____

RYRCA _____

NOSERP _____

TIRFS _____

WORD BANK

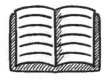 STORY

 DARK

 FIRST

 PERSON

 CARRY

 LEARN

UNSCRAMBLE THE R WORDS

The letters below are out of order! Unscramble the letters to make a word that has the R sound at the end. Write the word on the line. Then, practice saying the word 5 times. If you need a hint, look at the pictures at the bottom of the page. All of the scrambled words are pictured.

FINAL R
Level 1

IAHR _____

TETELR _____

RHEA _____

REHACET _____

OERST _____

IFER _____

— WORD BANK —

LETTER   FIRE   STORE   TEACHER   HEAR   HAIR

UNSCRAMBLE THE R WORDS

The letters below are out of order! Unscramble the letters to make a word that starts with R. Write the word on the line. Then, practice saying the word 5 times.

INITIAL R
Level 2

TOBRO _____

EPOR _____

GNPIPIR _____

BNOBIR _____

LOLR _____

AELR _____

SNIAIR _____

CACRONO _____

UNSCRAMBLE THE R WORDS

The letters below are out of order! Unscramble the letters to make a word that starts with R. Write the word on the line. Then practice saying the word 5 times.

INITIAL R
Level 2

KETCOR   _____

GLETANCER   _____

RTEMOE   _____

GRU   _____

SRESCE   _____

BITABR   _____

CORK   _____

NNNRIUG   _____

UNSCRAMBLE THE R WORDS

The letters below are out of order! Unscramble the letters to make a word that starts with R. Write the word on the line. Then practice saying the word 5 times.

INITIAL R
Level 2

HIGH FREQUENCY WORDS

NOSEAR _____

TULRES _____

THIGR _____

NURTRE _____

CHREAED _____

CEAR _____

GONIER _____

MORO _____

UNSCRAMBLE THE R WORDS

The letters below are out of order! Unscramble the letters to make a word that starts with R. Write the word on the line. Then practice saying the word 5 times.

INITIAL R
Level 2

HIGH FREQUENCY WORDS

MYTHHR   _____

TEAREP   _____

NAMEIR   _____

ESOR   _____

DEVIECER   _____

LUER   _____

OTOR   _____

DREI   _____

UNSCRAMBLE THE R WORDS

The letters below are out of order! Unscramble the letters to make an R sound in the middle of the word. Write the word on the line. Then, practice saying the word 5 times.

MEDIAL R
Level 2

HIGH FREQUENCY WORDS

SDWOR _____

RALNATU _____

LRIG _____

EHRAD _____

ECSFAUR _____

CCRILE _____

ERENYG _____

ECISXEER _____

UNSCRAMBLE THE R WORDS

The letters below are out of order! Unscramble the letters to make an R sound in the middle of the word. Write the word on the line. Then, practice saying the word 5 times.

MEDIAL R
Level 2

HIGH FREQUENCY WORDS

TERINTES _____

DRITH _____

GINNRUB _____

FLYOURES _____

RETCDI _____

VEERS _____

SERDET _____

NRRETCU _____

UNSCRAMBLE THE R WORDS

The letters below are out of order! Unscramble the letters to make an R sound in the middle of the word. Write the word on the line. Then, practice saying the word 5 times.

MEDIAL R
Level 2

YRREB _____

LUFERCA _____

NGROBI _____

IERRDMA _____

TORRPA _____

RINNTUG _____

TIPRAE _____

EIWRD _____

UNSCRAMBLE THE R WORDS

The letters below are out of order! Unscramble the letters to make an R sound in the middle of the word. Write the word on the line. Then, practice saying the word 5 times.

MEDIAL R
Level 2

SEROH _____

MAR _____

OKRF _____

RISHT _____

RIFAY _____

ZARLID _____

TYRAP _____

SUWARL _____

UNSCRAMBLE THE R WORDS

The letters below are out of order! Unscramble the letters to make a word that has the R sound at the end. Write the word on the line. Then, practice saying the word 5 times.

FINAL R
Level 2

HIGH FREQUENCY WORDS

EERW _____

THREO _____

ERH _____

OREV _____

TREAF _____

TTEELR _____

ERWI _____

IFER _____

UNSCRAMBLE THE R WORDS

The letters below are out of order! Unscramble the letters to make a word that has the R sound at the end. Write the word on the line. Then, practice saying the word 5 times.

FINAL R

Level 2

HIGH FREQUENCY WORDS

ERITH _____

TIRENE _____

SSTIER _____

CODORT _____

ERMMUS _____

TNIRWE _____

ROWPE _____

TTEARM _____

UNSCRAMBLE THE R WORDS

The letters below are out of order! Unscramble the letters to make a word that has the R sound at the end. Write the word on the line. Then, practice saying the word 5 times.

FINAL R
Level 2

OUFR _____

ERAB _____

ARJ _____

RHAIC _____

CRA _____

ERED _____

TERI _____

EROWFL _____

UNSCRAMBLE THE R WORDS

The letters below are out of order! Unscramble the letters to make a word that has the R sound at the end. Write the word on the line. Then, practice saying the word 5 times.

FINAL R
Level 2

RFATEH _____

NORUADIS _____

VAEBER _____

DDALER _____

THEROM _____

EITRTL _____

ONDERW _____

ERTTBE _____

UNSCRAMBLE THE R WORDS

The letters below are out of order! Unscramble the letters to make a word that has an initial R blend. Write the word on the line. Then, practice saying the word 5 times.

R BLENDS
Level 2

HIGH FREQUENCY WORDS

EAGRT _____

MFRO _____

REET _____

GORW _____

WADR _____

DCIER _____

NTOFR _____

NAIRT _____

UNSCRAMBLE THE R WORDS

The letters below are out of order! Unscramble the letters to make a word that has an initial R blend. Write the word on the line. Then, practice saying the word 5 times.

R BLENDS
Level 2

HIGH FREQUENCY WORDS

ROPD _____

TIRFU _____

VEIRD _____

COSSR _____

REEF _____

KBREA _____

ATRDE _____

WORCD _____

UNSCRAMBLE THE R WORDS

This is the answer key for Unscramble the R Words, Level 2.

INITIAL R

TOBRO	*ROBOT*	KETCOR	*ROCKET*
EPOR	*ROPE*	GLETANCER	*RECTANGLE*
GNPIPIR	*RIPPING*	RTEMOE	*REMOTE*
BNOBIR	*RIBBON*	GRU	*RUG*
LOLR	*ROLL*	SRESCE	*RECESS*
AELR	*REAL*	BITABR	*RABBIT*
SNIAIR	*RAISIN*	CORK	*ROCK*
CACRONO	*RACCOON*	NNNRIUG	*RUNNING*

NOSEAR	*REASON*	MYTHHR	*RHYTHM*
TULRES	*RESULT*	TEAREP	*REPEAT*
THIGR	*RIGHT*	NAMEIR	*REMAIN*
NURTRE	*RETURN*	ESOR	*ROSE*
CHREAED	*REACHED*	DEVIECER	*RECEIVED*
CEAR	*RACE*	LUER	*RULE*
GONIER	*REGION*	OTOR	*ROOT*
MORO	*ROOM*	DREI	*RIDE*

UNSCRAMBLE THE R WORDS

This is the answer key for Unscramble the R Words, Level 2.

MEDIAL R

SDWOR	*WORDS*	TERINTES	*INTEREST*
RALNATU	*NATURAL*	DRITH	*THIRD*
LRIG	*GIRL*	GINNRUB	*BURNING*
EHRAD	*HEARD*	FLYOURES	*YOURSELF*
ECSFAUR	*SURFACE*	RETCDI	*DIRECT*
CCRILE	*CIRCLE*	VEERS	*SERVE*
ERENYG	*ENERGY*	SERDET	*DESERT*
ECISXEER	*EXERCISE*	NRRETCU	*CURRENT*

YRREB	*BERRY*	SEROH	*HORSE*
LUFERCA	*CAREFUL*	MAR	*ARM*
NGROBI	*BORING*	OKRF	*FORK*
IERRDMA	*MARRIED*	RISHT	*SHIRT*
TORRPA	*PARROT*	RIFAY	*FAIRY*
RINNTUG	*TURNING*	ZARLID	*LIZARD*
TIPRAE	*PIRATE*	TYRAP	*PARTY*
EIWRD	*WEIRD*	SUWARL	*WALRUS*

UNSCRAMBLE THE R WORDS

This is the answer key for Unscramble the R Words, Level 2.

FINAL R

EERW	*WERE*	ERITH	*THEIR*
THREO	*OTHER*	TIRENE	*ENTIRE*
ERH	*HER*	SSTIER	*SISTER*
OREV	*OVER*	CODORT	*DOCTOR*
TREAF	*AFTER*	ERMMUS	*SUMMER*
TTEELR	*LETTER*	TNIRWE	*WINTER*
ERWI	*WIRE*	ROWPE	*POWER*
IFER	*FIRE*	TTEARM	*MATTER*

OUFR	*FOUR*	RFATEH	*FATHER*
ERAB	*BEAR*	NORUADIS	*DINOSAUR*
ARJ	*JAR*	VAEBER	*BEAVER*
RHAIC	*CHAIR*	DDALER	*LADDER*
CRA	*CAR*	THEROM	*MOTHER*
ERED	*DEER*	EITRTL	*LITTER*
TERI	*TIRE*	ONDERW	*WONDER*
EROWFL	*FLOWER*	ERTTBE	*BETTER*

UNSCRAMBLE THE R WORDS

This is the answer key for Unscramble the R Words, Level 2.

R BLENDS

EAGRT	*GREAT*	ROPD	*DROP*
MFRO	*FROM*	TIRFU	*FRUIT*
REET	*TREE*	VEIRD	*DRIVE*
GORW	*GROW*	COSSR	*CROSS*
WADR	*DRAW*	REEF	*FREE*
DCIER	*CRIED*	KBREA	*BREAK*
NTOFR	*FRONT*	ATRDE	*TRADE*
NAIRT	*TRAIN*	WORCD	*CROWD*

264

WORD SEARCH

Read the words in the word bank. Say each word ten times. Find those words in the word search below and circle them. When you find the word, practice saying it again.

INITIAL R

```
Q M A R O B O T F A N P
S E B U A K I Z L R R O
C V B N M C T U O P E N
A R S D R R E L W O I D
W H R P R I N C E R I N
R Y N R I N S E R R E N
O M E E B S O M R I L K
R E R A L G R O C K E T
O R I D I R H Y U H R J
A E S Y N L O V E R O V
D I T R K I D P R W Z S
R E S P O N S I B L E A
```

WORD BANK

ROBOT
RACE

RUN
RED
RINSE

READY
ROAD
ROCKET

RESPONSIBLE
RHYME

ALL RIGHTS RESERVED © 2017 PEACHIESPEECHIE.COM

265

WORD SEARCH

Read the words in the word bank. Say each word ten times. Find those words in the word search below and circle them. When you find the word, practice saying it again.

INITIAL R ANSWER KEY

```
Q M A R O B O T F A N P
S E B U A K I Z L R R O
C V B N M C T U O P E N
A R S D R R E L W O I D
W H R P R I N C E R I N
R Y N R I N S E R R E N
O Y M E E B S O M R I L K
R E R A L G R O C K E T
O R I D I R H Y U H R J
A E S Y N L O V E R O V
D I T R K I D P R W Z S
R E S P O N S I B L E A
```

WORD BANK

ROBOT
RACE

RUN
RED
RINSE

READY
ROAD
ROCKET

RESPONSIBLE
RHYME

WORD SEARCH

Read the words in the word bank. Say each word ten times. Find those words in the word search below and circle them. When you find the word, practice saying it again.

MEDIAL R

```
C A R R Y O E A B M B C
L O V E K I A N D P E L
C F R I C A R R O T R E
E N D D A N R C E R R H
R Y M B O R I N G S I N
E G O O D R N I K H E T
A Y U M O R G E A F S Z
L B X N Q I B L O I P S
R P A R E N T O R R O R
C G A R A H K J Q S W V
A O I S N A E Q D T P Z
R P E R S O N T Y R F A
```

WORD BANK

CARRY
EARRING

BARN
PERSON
FIRST

BERRIES
PARENT
BORING

CARROT
CEREAL

WORD SEARCH

Read the words in the word bank. Say each word ten times. Find those words in the word search below and circle them. When you find the word, practice saying it again.

MEDIAL R ANSWER KEY

```
C A R R Y O E A B M B C
L O V E K I A N D P E L
C F R I C A R R O T R E
E N D D A N R C E R R H
R Y M B O R I N G S I N
E G O O D R N I K H E T
A Y U M O R G E A F S Z
L B X N Q I B L O I P S
R P A R E N T O R R O R
C G A R A H K J Q S W V
A O I S N A E Q D T P Z
R P E R S O N T Y R F A
```

WORD BANK

CARRY
EARRING

BARN
PERSON
FIRST

BERRIES
PARENT
BORING

CARROT
CEREAL

WORD SEARCH

Read the words in the word bank. Say each word ten times. Find those words in the word search below and circle them. When you find the word, practice saying it again.

FINAL R

```
A C E T H E R E I T A F
T B A B L O V E A N D I
H H R T Y D O O R A S R
A E K I N D N E S S U E
I R Q W D E L M C Z N J
R T E A E R O R V A K Q
Z S R H A X V D O X R P
Q W H E R E C E H U G S
S A M E E Q H S A L A R
A U N T T E A C H E R Q
V H E L P S I E R F Z H
E L E T T E R K I E R E
```

WORD BANK

THERE	WHERE	FIRE	DOOR
HER	DEAR	TEACHER	LETTER
	CAR	CHAIR	

WORD SEARCH

Read the words in the word bank. Say each word ten times. Find those words in the word search below and circle them. When you find the word, practice saying it again.

FINAL R ANSWER KEY

```
A  C  E  T  H  E  R  E  I  T  A  F
T  B  A  B  L  O  V  E  A  N  D  I
H  H  R  T  Y  D  O  O  R  A  S  R
A  E  K  I  N  D  N  E  S  S  U  E
I  R  Q  W  D  E  L  M  C  Z  N  J
R  T  E  A  E  R  O  R  V  A  K  Q
Z  S  R  H  A  X  V  D  O  X  R  P
Q  W  H  E  R  E  C  E  H  U  G  S
S  A  M  E  E  Q  H  S  A  L  A  R
A  U  N  T  T  E  A  C  H  E  R  Q
V  H  E  L  P  S  I  E  R  F  Z  H
E  L  E  T  T  E  R  K  I  E  R  E
```

WORD BANK

THERE	WHERE	FIRE	DOOR
HER	DEAR	TEACHER	LETTER
	CAR	CHAIR	

WORD SEARCH

Read the words in the word bank. Say each word ten times. Find those words in the word search below and circle them. When you find the word, practice saying it again.

R BLENDS

```
B L I N K I N D N E S S
F R O M G X D R L A Q Z
G M I R F T R U C K H C
R R E N R E I M R E J R
I D G R G X V F Y H L B
T R Y A T A E K B L R R
L J K F Q W T E R Y U A
S P R E T T Y L I N O V
P R O G R O W I N G G E
A T A X Z K R T R U R N
F R I E N D H E I F D H
T D H G F R W P R O U D
```

WORD BANK

TRY	DRIVE	GROWING	PROUD
BRING	TRUCK	BRAVE	PRETTY
	CRY	FRIEND	

WORD SEARCH

Read the words in the word bank. Say each word ten times. Find those words in the word search below and circle them. When you find the word, practice saying it again.

R BLENDS ANSWER KEY

```
B L I N K I N D N E S S
F R O M G X D R L A Q Z
G M I R F T R U C K H C
R R E N R E I M R E J R
I D G R G X V F Y H L B
T R Y A T A E K B L R R
L J K F Q W T E R Y U A
S P R E T T Y L I N O V
P R O G R O W I N G G E
A T A X Z K R T R U R N
F R I E N D H E I F D H
T D H G F R W P R O U D
```

WORD BANK

TRY
BRING
DRIVE
TRUCK
CRY
GROWING
BRAVE
FRIEND
PROUD
PRETTY

I CAN SAY THE R SOUND!

The R Sound in Two-Word Phrases

Say each phrase below. Be sure to use your good R sound. Say each phrase 5 times, checking a box each time you do it.

HEAVY RAIN ☐ ☐ ☐ ☐ ☐

METAL ROBOT ☐ ☐ ☐ ☐ ☐

CHEWY RAISINS ☐ ☐ ☐ ☐ ☐

SOFT RABBIT ☐ ☐ ☐ ☐ ☐

LONG RIBBON ☐ ☐ ☐ ☐ ☐

I CAN SAY THE R SOUND!

The R Sound in Two-Word Phrases   **Initial R**

Say each phrase below. Be sure to use your good R sound. Say each phrase 5 times, checking a box each time you do it.

SMALL RAT   ☐ ☐ ☐ ☐ ☐

HARD ROCK   ☐ ☐ ☐ ☐ ☐

NICE RING   ☐ ☐ ☐ ☐ ☐

FAST ROCKET   ☐ ☐ ☐ ☐ ☐

BIG RACE   ☐ ☐ ☐ ☐ ☐

I CAN SAY THE R SOUND!

The R Sound in Two-Word Phrases

Medial R

Say each phrase below. Be sure to use your good R sound. Say each phrase 5 times, checking a box each time you do it.

LITTLE FARM ☐ ☐ ☐ ☐ ☐

ORANGE CARROT ☐ ☐ ☐ ☐ ☐

GOLD EARRINGS ☐ ☐ ☐ ☐ ☐

SWEET CEREAL ☐ ☐ ☐ ☐ ☐

GOOD MORNING ☐ ☐ ☐ ☐ ☐

I CAN SAY THE R SOUND!

The R Sound in Two-Word Phrases

Medial R

Say each phrase below. Be sure to use your good R sound. Say each phrase 5 times, checking a box each time you do it.

I'M BORED ☐ ☐ ☐ ☐ ☐

SHOPPING CART ☐ ☐ ☐ ☐ ☐

MILK CARTON ☐ ☐ ☐ ☐ ☐

LOUD SIREN ☐ ☐ ☐ ☐ ☐

NICE PERSON ☐ ☐ ☐ ☐ ☐

I CAN SAY THE R SOUND!

The R Sound in Two-Word Phrases

Final R

Say each phrase below. Be sure to use your good R sound. Say each phrase 5 times, checking a box each time you do it.

HOT FIRE ☐ ☐ ☐ ☐ ☐

HAPPY DEER ☐ ☐ ☐ ☐ ☐

FAST CAR ☐ ☐ ☐ ☐ ☐

YELLOW STAR ☐ ☐ ☐ ☐ ☐

SOFT FUR ☐ ☐ ☐ ☐ ☐

I CAN SAY THE R SOUND!

The R Sound in Two-Word Phrases   Final R

Say each phrase below. Be sure to use your good R sound. Say each phrase 5 times, checking a box each time you do it.

HELLO SIR ☐ ☐ ☐ ☐ ☐

OPEN DOOR ☐ ☐ ☐ ☐ ☐

NEW TIRE ☐ ☐ ☐ ☐ ☐

CANDY BAR ☐ ☐ ☐ ☐ ☐

LOUD PURR ☐ ☐ ☐ ☐ ☐

I CAN SAY THE R SOUND!

The R Sound in Two-Word Phrases   **R-Blends**

Say each phrase below. Be sure to use your good R sound. Say each phrase 5 times, checking a box each time you do it.

EAT GRAPES   ☐ ☐ ☐ ☐ ☐

TALL TREE   ☐ ☐ ☐ ☐ ☐

OPEN PRESENT   ☐ ☐ ☐ ☐ ☐

LOUD DRUM   ☐ ☐ ☐ ☐ ☐

PINK DRESS   ☐ ☐ ☐ ☐ ☐

I CAN SAY THE R SOUND!

The R Sound in Two-Word Phrases

R-Blends

Say each phrase below. Be sure to use your good R sound. Say each phrase 5 times, checking a box each time you do it.

STINKY TRASH ☐ ☐ ☐ ☐ ☐

BIG TRUCK ☐ ☐ ☐ ☐ ☐

HOT GRILL ☐ ☐ ☐ ☐ ☐

COLD DRINK ☐ ☐ ☐ ☐ ☐

WHITE BREAD ☐ ☐ ☐ ☐ ☐

CARRIER PHRASE FUN! | INITIAL R

Say the phrase "I see a _____" along with the R words listed. Remember to move your tongue into the correct position when you say the R sound.

I see a _____.

RADIO

RABBIT

ROCK

RING

RHINO

ROLL

ROBOT

RIBBON

RAT

ROAD

CARRIER PHRASE FUN!

Say the phrase "I see a _____" along with the R words listed. Remember to move your tongue into the correct position when you say the R sound.

I see a _____.

HERO

FERRET

PARENT

EARRING

BERRY

PIRATE

SIREN

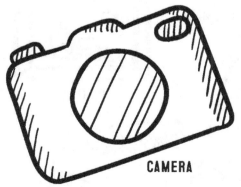

CAMERA

PARROT

CARROT

CARRIER PHRASE FUN!

FINAL R

Say the phrase "I see a _____" along with the R words listed. Remember to move your tongue into the correct position when you say the R sound.

I see a _____.

HELICOPTER

SHOWER

FATHER

DIGGER

FEATHER

PICTURE

THEATER

MOTHER

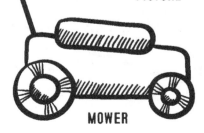

MOWER

HAMSTER

I CAN SAY THE R SOUND!

Directions: Say each sentence below. Color the picture after you say the sentence.

INITIAL R

I <u>rode</u> my bike down the sidewalk.

I hope it doesn't <u>rain</u> on Tuesday.

We painted the walls <u>red</u>.

My cousin has a fluffy pet <u>rat</u>.

Did you see the <u>rainbow</u> in the sky?

I CAN SAY THE R SOUND!

Directions: Say each sentence below. Color the picture after you say the sentence.

 Mom packed a box of <u>raisins</u> in my lunch.

 David twisted his <u>wrist</u> in gymnastics class.

 I put the <u>rose</u> in a vase on the table.

 Did you eat <u>rice</u> for lunch?

 I accidentally <u>ripped</u> one of the pages in my book.

I CAN SAY THE R SOUND!

Directions: Say each sentence below. Color the picture after you say the sentence.

INITIAL ER

 <u>Ernie</u> packed his bags for vacation.

 I <u>earned</u> money by mowing my uncle's lawn.

 We had to wake up <u>early</u> to catch the school bus.

 I learned about the planet <u>Earth</u> in science class.

 My mom's name is <u>Irma</u>.

I CAN SAY THE R SOUND!

Directions: Say each sentence below. Color the picture after you say the sentence.

MEDIAL ER

Are you <u>nervous</u> about taking the math test?

My cat is <u>furry</u> and sweet.

I bought a package of <u>paperclips</u> today.

We <u>learned</u> a lot in social studies class.

I chopped <u>turnips</u> for my salad.

I CAN SAY THE R SOUND!

Directions: Say each sentence below. Color the picture after you say the sentence.

FINAL ER

You should <u>stir</u> the hot oatmeal.

The balloons belong to <u>her</u>.

I love to play <u>soccer</u> with my cousins.

We saw a <u>helicopter</u> in the sky.

She found a <u>feather</u> while she was playing outside.

I CAN SAY THE R SOUND!

Directions: Say each sentence below. Color the picture after you say the sentence.

INITIAL AR

My dad was in the <u>army</u>.

My <u>artwork</u> is hanging on the wall.

The <u>aardvark</u> is looking for food.

She is a talented <u>artist</u>.

Sometimes my aunt and uncle <u>argue</u>.

I CAN SAY THE R SOUND!

Directions: Say each sentence below. Color the picture after you say the sentence.

 Many animals live in the <u>barn</u>.

 I bought a <u>carton</u> of milk today.

 She used to live on a <u>farm</u>.

 Push the <u>cart</u> down the aisle.

 The <u>martian</u> is visiting us this weekend.

I CAN SAY THE R SOUND!

Directions: Say each sentence below. Color the picture after you say the sentence.

 Look at the shining <u>star</u> in the sky.

 Please help me open the <u>jar</u> of jelly.

 What a lovely new <u>car</u>!

 Watch out! The <u>tar</u> is sticky.

 I bought a chocolate candy <u>bar</u>.

I CAN SAY THE R SOUND!

Directions: Say each sentence below. Color the picture after you say the sentence.

INITIAL EAR

She loves the new <u>earrings</u>.

I like to listen to music with my <u>earphones</u>.

She was feeling <u>irritated</u> this evening.

Listen to that <u>eerie</u> music!

They have an <u>irrigation</u> system.

I CAN SAY THE R SOUND!

Directions: Say each sentence below. Color the picture after you say the sentence.

My niece just got her nose <u>pierced</u>.

I like eating <u>cereal</u> for lunch.

You must put a <u>period</u> at the end of a sentence.

My dad has a long bushy <u>beard</u>.

I bought a comic book about a magical <u>hero</u>.

I CAN SAY THE R SOUND!

Directions: Say each sentence below. Color the picture after you say the sentence.

FINAL EAR

A <u>tear</u> slid down his cheek.

I saw a <u>deer</u> eating plants outside my window.

The sky was <u>clear</u> and blue.

She likes to <u>volunteer</u> at the school.

I know how to <u>steer</u> my bike.

I CAN SAY THE R SOUND!

Directions: Say each sentence below. Color the picture after you say the sentence.

INITIAL IRE

 I know a boy who lives in <u>Ireland</u>.

 My mom <u>irons</u> the clothes each day.

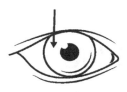 Part of my eye is called an <u>iris</u>.

 I met a kind <u>Irish</u> leprechaun.

 <u>Irene</u> loves to wear polka-dots.

I CAN SAY THE R SOUND!

Directions: Say each sentence below. Color the picture after you say the sentence.

MEDIAL IRE

We used <u>pliers</u> to fix the sink.

I went to bed at six o'clock because I was so <u>tired</u>.

Let's go outside and get some <u>firewood</u>.

Did you see the <u>pirate</u> flag?

The <u>siren</u> was loud.

I CAN SAY THE R SOUND!

Directions: Say each sentence below. Color the picture after you say the sentence.

FINAL IRE

I will put out the <u>fire</u>.

I need a piece of <u>wire</u> for my project.

I put a new <u>tire</u> on my bike.

Did you see the <u>flyer</u> on the wall?

I was a <u>vampire</u> for Halloween.

I CAN SAY THE R SOUND!

Directions: Say each sentence below. Color the picture after you say the sentence.

 I stood by the <u>air</u> vent because it was nice and cool.

 <u>Aaron</u> loves to spend time with his family.

 I took an <u>airplane</u> to visit Aunt Becky.

 Please take me to the <u>airport</u>.

 If you are lost, just follow the <u>arrow</u>.

I CAN SAY THE R SOUND!

Directions: Say each sentence below. Color the picture after you say the sentence.

The <u>parrot</u> knows how to talk.

We got <u>married</u> last weekend.

I fed my pet bunny a <u>carrot</u>.

Why are you <u>wearing</u> a silly hat?

We are <u>sharing</u> a milkshake.

I CAN SAY THE R SOUND!

Directions: Say each sentence below. Color the picture after you say the sentence.

FINAL AIR

I didn't mean to <u>tear</u> the page from the magazine.

This is a juicy delicious <u>pear</u>.

The <u>bear</u> is looking for a snack.

Her <u>hair</u> is very long.

The ball is right <u>there</u>.

I CAN SAY THE R SOUND!

Directions: Say each sentence below. Color the picture after you say the sentence.

INITIAL OR

 I ate an <u>orange</u> for lunch.

 We only eat <u>organic</u> vegetables.

 Hang the <u>ornament</u> on the tree.

 Have you been to <u>Oregon</u>?

 Look at the apples in the <u>orchard</u>.

I CAN SAY THE R SOUND!

Directions: Say each sentence below. Color the picture after you say the sentence.

MEDIAL OR

 He ate <u>corn</u> for lunch.

 I was <u>bored</u> at school today.

 We saw a <u>horse</u> in a field.

 I watched a movie this <u>morning</u>.

 She made a <u>fortune</u> selling paintings.

I CAN SAY THE R SOUND!

Directions: Say each sentence below. Color the picture after you say the sentence.

FINAL OR

 I went shopping at the <u>store</u>.

 I will <u>pour</u> the paint into the bucket.

 She is almost <u>four</u> years old.

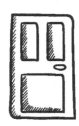 Open the <u>door</u> and let me in.

 He likes to sit on the <u>floor</u>.

I CAN SAY THE R SOUND!

Directions: Say each sentence below. Color the picture after you say the sentence.

R BLENDS

 I baked a loaf of <u>bread</u> today.

 We walked along the <u>trail</u>.

 Put the tissues in the <u>trash</u> can.

 The <u>truck</u> was speeding down the highway.

 I am learning to play the <u>drums</u>.

SILLY R SENTENCES: READ AND ILLUSTRATE

INITIAL
R

Say the sentences below using your best R sound. Then, illustrate the silly scene in the space provided.

Rachel put a red ribbon on her pet rat.

The heavy rhino rocked the rickety rowboat.

The rabbit wore ruby rings on his toes.

SILLY R SENTENCES: READ AND ILLUSTRATE | INITIAL R

Say the sentences below using your best R sound. Then, illustrate the silly scene in the space provided.

The reindeer raced the plane down the runway.

The red robin went down the river in a raft.

The robot rolled down the street on roller skates.

SILLY R SENTENCES: READ AND ILLUSTRATE | INITIAL R

Say the sentences below using your best R sound. Then, illustrate the silly scene in the space provided.

Ricky rode his rocking horse down River Street.

Rebekah rides her bike while wearing a robe.

Ryan and Rob ate ten roast beef sandwiches.

SILLY R SENTENCES: READ AND ILLUSTRATE

INITIAL R

Say the sentences below using your best R sound. Then, illustrate the silly scene in the space provided.

The radio was ringing loudly at the rodeo.

The raccoon bought red roses for his aunt.

I ate raisins on my flying rug.

SILLY R SENTENCES: READ AND ILLUSTRATE

Say the sentences below using your best R sound. Then, illustrate the silly scene in the space provided.

Renee used a remote to stop the rain.

Rowan cooked rice on the roof top.

The rich receptionist bought 100 bottles of ranch dressing.

SILLY R SENTENCES: READ AND ILLUSTRATE | MEDIAL R

Say the sentences below using your best R sound. Then, illustrate the silly scene in the space provided.

The turkey sat in a carseat on the airplane.

The fireman had a siren on his overalls.

The girls were cheering about getting popcorn.

SILLY R SENTENCES: READ AND ILLUSTRATE | MEDIAL R

Say the sentences below using your best R sound. Then, illustrate the silly scene in the space provided.

The pirates caught starfish and fed them carrots.

Carla planted paperclips in her garden.

The person eating a corndog has a pet parrot.

SILLY R SENTENCES: READ AND ILLUSTRATE | MEDIAL R

Say the sentences below using your best R sound. Then, illustrate the silly scene in the space provided.

The curtains had surfboards and hearts on them.

Bertha surfed around the pyramids.

The worms were carrying acorns to the squirrels.

SILLY R SENTENCES: READ AND ILLUSTRATE

MEDIAL R

Say the sentences below using your best R sound. Then, illustrate the silly scene in the space provided.

Barron was watering his pet turtle in the yard.

The walrus ate syrup with carrots each morning.

The giraffe went to the park with the lizard.

SILLY R SENTENCES: READ AND ILLUSTRATE

FINAL R

Say the sentences below using your best R sound. Then, illustrate the silly scene in the space provided.

The hamster played soccer in the shower.

Father made a hat out of newspaper.

Mother likes to stare at her lawn mower.

SILLY R SENTENCES: READ AND ILLUSTRATE

FINAL R

Say the sentences below using your best R sound. Then, illustrate the silly scene in the space provided.

The doctor played the guitar while eating a s'more.

Peter can hear the deer using a hammer.

The police officer played soccer in the theater.

SILLY R SENTENCES: READ AND ILLUSTRATE | FINAL R

Say the sentences below using your best R sound. Then, illustrate the silly scene in the space provided.

The farmer wore his bathing suit outside in the winter weather.

The teacher flew a helicopter to school.

The juggler and the clown live together in a tower.

SILLY R SENTENCES: READ AND ILLUSTRATE

Say the sentences below using your best R sound. Then, illustrate the silly scene in the space provided.

Father took a picture of a puppy in a stroller.

The beaver picked a flower for his father.

The alligator chased the bear up the ladder.

SILLY R SENTENCES: READ AND ILLUSTRATE | R BLENDS

Say the sentences below using your best R sound. Then, illustrate the silly scene in the space provided.

Grandpa fed grapes to his pet crab.

The baby dragon cried in his crib.

The frog drove his tractor to the grocery store.

SILLY R SENTENCES: READ AND ILLUSTRATE

R BLENDS

Say the sentences below using your best R sound. Then, illustrate the silly scene in the space provided.

The prince gave pretzels to all of his friends.

My brother grilled fruit for breakfast.

Brandy's Christmas present was a truck full of prunes.

SILLY R SENTENCES: READ AND ILLUSTRATE

R BLENDS

Say the sentences below using your best R sound. Then, illustrate the silly scene in the space provided.

Gretta's freckles are shaped like triangles.

Princess Priscilla drives a tractor.

I dreamed about drinking fruit juice from a treasure chest.

SYNONYM SEARCH

Read the sentences below. Replace the underlined word with a synonym that starts with the R sound. Write the synonym on the line and practice saying it with your best R sound.

INITIAL R

—— WORD BANK ——

ready	rip	rocks
wreck	repair	road

1. Polly was in a car <u>crash</u> last weekend, but she is okay. _____

2. Did you <u>tear</u> the paper in half? _____

3. I held my dad's hand as we walked across the <u>street</u>. _____

4. My cousin helped me <u>fix</u> the broken toy. _____

5. We found several large <u>stones</u> in the backyard. _____

6. Are you <u>prepared</u> for the big performance? _____

SYNONYM SEARCH

Read the sentences below. Replace the underlined word with a synonym that has the R sound in the middle. Write the synonym on the line and practice saying it with your best R sound.

MEDIAL R

— WORD BANK —

hard	start	large
terrible	weird	dirty

1. I'm not going to school today because I feel <u>awful</u>. _____

2. That math test was <u>difficult</u>! _____

3. After going camping, my shoes were <u>filthy</u>. _____

4. My mom made a <u>big</u> pizza for dinner. _____

5. My grandma's cat looks <u>odd</u>. _____

6. The party will <u>begin</u> at five o'clock. _____

SYNONYM SEARCH

Read the sentences below. Replace the underlined word with a synonym that has the R sound at the end. Write the synonym on the line and practice saying it with your best R sound.

FINAL R

WORD BANK

picture	clever	under
car	store	shear

1. My uncle wants to buy a new <u>automobile</u>. _____

2. The cat hid <u>beneath</u> the stairs. _____

3. We bought gloves at a local <u>shop</u>. _____

4. Farmer John needs to <u>shave</u> the sheep. _____

5. My cousin Amy is <u>smart</u>. _____

6. I looked at a <u>photo</u> of my mom. _____

SYNONYM SEARCH

Read the sentences below. Replace the underlined word with a synonym that has an initial R blend. Write the synonym on the line and practice saying it with your best R sound.

R BLENDS

WORD BANK

pretty	cried	great
grabbed	tripped	friends

1. He is one of my closest <u>pals</u>. _____

2. We had a <u>wonderful</u> time at the party. _____

3. I <u>stumbled</u> over a rock in the grass. _____

4. The toddler <u>snatched</u> the toy out of my hands. _____

5. She wore a <u>beautiful</u> dress to the ball. _____

6. The little boy <u>sobbed</u> after falling on the playground. _____

ANTONYM SEARCH

Read the sentences below. Replace the underlined word with an antonym that has the R sound at the beginning. Write the antonym on the line and practice saying it with your best R sound.

INITIAL R

WORD BANK

rotten	run	real
rude	rapidly	raise

1. We <u>walk</u> in the hallways. _____

2. I saw a <u>fake</u> unicorn at the mall. _____

3. The dolphin moved <u>slowly</u> through the sea. _____

4. My teacher told me to <u>lower</u> my hand. _____

5. He is known for being <u>polite</u>. _____

6. The fruit at the market looks <u>fresh</u>. _____

ANTONYM SEARCH

Read the sentences below. Replace the underlined word with an antonym that has the R sound in the middle. Write the antonym on the line and practice saying it with your best R sound.

MEDIAL R

WORD BANK

apart   terrible   worst

furry   dangerous   start

1. Aunt Tina has a <u>hairless</u> cat. _____

2. We had a <u>great</u> vacation. _____

3. Papa's Cafe makes the <u>best</u> pizza in town. _____

4. Please <u>stop</u> singing that song. _____

5. This is a <u>safe</u> place to go camping. _____

6. They have been living <u>together</u> for six months. _____

ANTONYM SEARCH

Read the sentences below. Replace the underlined word with an antonym that has the R sound at the end. Write the antonym on the line and practice saying it with your best R sound.

FINAL R

— WORD BANK —

more	bitter	failure
lower	younger	clear

1. She is a few months <u>older</u> than me. _____

2. This coffee tastes <u>sweet</u>. _____

3. We talked about her recent <u>success</u> at school. _____

4. Everything looked <u>blurry</u> when I put on the glasses. _____

5. Let's <u>raise</u> the flag in the yard. _____

6. I spent <u>less</u> time with my mom last week. _____

ANTONYM SEARCH

Read the sentences below. Replace the underlined word with an antonym that has an initial R blend in it. Write the antonym on the line and practice saying it with your best R sound.

R BLENDS

WORD BANK

bright	friend	pretty
dry	crooked	create

1. Grandma's brown cat is <u>ugly</u>. _____

2. The light in the kitchen is <u>dim</u>. _____

3. I am going to <u>destroy</u> a block tower. _____

4. Her boots are <u>wet</u>. _____

5. He has been my <u>enemy</u> for a long time. _____

6. The children were in a <u>straight</u> line. _____

STORY TIME | INITIAL R

Read the story aloud. Be sure to use your best R sound! Then, answer the questions about the story and illustrate it in the space provided.

REBECCA AND RYAN

Rebecca lives in Rhode Island. Rebecca loves outdoor activities such as bike riding and roller skating. Rebecca often rides her bike to her best friend Ryan's house. Ryan has a pet rat named Ricky. When Rebecca visits Ryan, they like to watch Ricky run around in his cage.

ILLUSTRATE THE STORY

WHO ARE THE CHARACTERS IN THIS STORY?

WHAT ACTIVITIES DOES REBECCA ENJOY?

WHERE DOES REBECCA OFTEN RIDE HER BIKE?

WHAT IS RYAN'S PET'S NAME?

WHAT DOES RICKY DO IN HIS CAGE?

329

STORY TIME — INITIAL R

Read the story aloud. Be sure to use your best R sound! Then, answer the questions about the story and illustrate it in the space provided.

ROCKY THE RHINO

Rocky is a large gray rhinoceros that lives in the Red River Zoo. Rocky's gray skin blends in with the rocks in his pen, which is how he got his name! Rocky really enjoys playing with the other rhinos at the zoo. When he gets sleepy, he rests in the grass near the rocks. The people that visit the Red River Zoo love taking pictures of Rocky the rhinoceros.

ILLUSTRATE THE STORY

WHAT KIND OF ANIMAL IS ROCKY?

WHERE DOES ROCKY LIVE?

HOW DID ROCKY GET HIS NAME?

WHAT DOES ROCKY ENJOY DOING?

WHAT DOES ROCKY DO WHEN HE GETS SLEEPY?

STORY TIME

MEDIAL R

Read the story aloud. Be sure to use your best R sound! Then, answer the questions about the story and illustrate it in the space provided.

SATURDAY MORNING FUN

Carla woke up early one Saturday morning and went downstairs. She poured herself a bowl of cereal to eat. As Carla ate her cereal, she watched cartoons on television. Carla's pet parrot, Terence, sat next to her and watched cartoons as well. Carla shared some of her cereal with Terence. Carla and her parrot enjoy eating cereal and watching cartoons every Saturday morning.

ILLUSTRATE THE STORY

WHEN DID THIS STORY TAKE PLACE?

WHAT DID CARLA EAT FOR BREAKFAST?

WHAT DID CARLA WATCH ON TELEVISION?

WHAT KIND OF PET DOES CARLA HAVE?

WHAT IS CARLA'S PET'S NAME?

MEDIAL R

Read the story aloud. Be sure to use your best R sound! Then, answer the questions about the story and illustrate it in the space provided.

CARROT CAKE SURPRISE

Karen was preparing for her cousin Mary's surprise birthday party. Karen was baking Mary a carrot cake. Mary was turning thirty, and carrot cake has always been her favorite! As Karen was baking, she ran out of carrots! Karen went to see her neighbor, Barney. She asked him if she could borrow some carrots. Barney gave Karen several carrots. Karen finished the cake just in time. Mary loved her birthday surprise!

ILLUSTRATE THE STORY

WHAT WAS KAREN PREPARING FOR?

WHAT KIND OF CAKE IS MARY'S FAVORITE?

HOW OLD WAS MARY TURNING?

WHAT PROBLEM DID KAREN HAVE IN THE STORY?

WHO HELPED KAREN?

STORY TIME

FINAL R

Read the story aloud. Be sure to use your best R sound! Then, answer the questions about the story and illustrate it in the space provided.

PETER PLAYS SOCCER

It was a hot summer day and Peter was playing a game of soccer with his friends. Peter's little sister, Heather, always watches his soccer games. She likes to clap and cheer when Peter kicks the soccer ball into the goal. With Heather watching and cheering, Peter's team won the game! Heather gave Peter a high five. Peter took a cold shower after the game to cool off.

ILLUSTRATE THE STORY

IN WHAT SEASON DID THIS STORY TAKE PLACE?

WHAT GAME WAS PETER PLAYING?

WHO WATCHES PETER'S GAMES?

WHAT DOES HEATHER DO WHEN PETER KICKS THAT BALL INTO THE GOAL?

WHAT DID PETER DO AFTER THE GAME?

STORY TIME

FINAL R

Read the story aloud. Be sure to use your best R sound! Then, answer the questions about the story and illustrate it in the space provided.

CLASS PET

There once was a black and grey hamster named Pepper. Pepper lived in a classroom as a class pet. His cage was in the back corner of the classroom on a table. The teacher and students in the class took care of him. They gave Pepper water to drink. They gave Pepper food to eat. They let Pepper out to play on the big chair in the classroom. Every day, the teacher put a star sticker on the chart to show that they had taken care of Pepper.

ILLUSTRATE THE STORY

WHAT KIND OF ANIMAL WAS PEPPER?

WHO TOOK CARE OF PEPPER?

WHAT DID PEPPER DRINK?

WHERE WAS PEPPER'S CAGE?

WHAT DID THE TEACHER USE TO SHOW THAT THEY TOOK CARE OF PEPPER?

334

R BLENDS

Read the story aloud. Be sure to use your best R sound! Then, answer the questions about the story and illustrate it in the space provided.

CRANKY THE CRAB

Cranky was a crab that lived on the beach. His name was Cranky because he was always in a bad mood. Cranky wasn't like the other crabs. He was green instead of red! And he had little freckles all over his shell. Cranky didn't like being different. One day, he was crawling along the sand, eating bits of bread and fruit, when another crab approached him. "You are such a lovely green color!" said the other crab. That made Cranky smile. He wasn't as cranky after that!

ILLUSTRATE THE STORY

WHAT KIND OF ANIMAL WAS CRANKY?

WHERE DID CRANKY LIVE?

WHAT MADE CRANKY DIFFERENT FROM THE OTHER CRABS?

WHAT DID CRANKY EAT?

WHAT MADE CRANKY SMILE?

CARRYOVER ACTIVITY: DESCRIBING

MIXED WORD POSITIONS

Once you can say the R sound in speech therapy, it is important to work on carrying that skill over to connected speech/conversation. Even if you can say the R sound perfectly in sentences, it can be tricky to remember it when you are chatting with your friends. This activity will help you practice your R sound in connected speech.

Directions: You will talk about the items listed below. You will describe them in detail. Be sure to think about your R sound while you are talking. Some R words you may want to use have been listed for you. Once you're done, rate how you think you did by marking one of the faces.

Ball	round recess run rolls	_Example_ A ball is <u>r</u>ound and it <u>r</u>olls. You can play with a ball at <u>r</u>ecess. You can kick a ball and <u>r</u>un after it.
Car	drive faster turn race	☹ 😐 🙂 😀
School	learn write read teacher	☹ 😐 🙂 😀
Candy	wrapper sour red crunchy	☹ 😐 🙂 😀
Video Game	controller player rules screen	☹ 😐 🙂 😀
Crayons	color write orange paper	☹ 😐 🙂 😀

CARRYOVER ACTIVITY: DESCRIBING

MIXED WORD POSITIONS

Once you can say the R sound in speech therapy, it is important to work on carrying that skill over to connected speech/conversation. Even if you can say the R sound perfectly in sentences, it can be tricky to remember it when you are chatting with your friends. This activity will help you practice your R sound in connected speech.

Directions: You will talk about the items/events listed below. You will describe them in detail. Be sure to think about your R sound while you are talking. Once you're done, rate how you think you did by marking one of the faces.

Circus	☹ 😐 🙂 😀
Homework	☹ 😐 🙂 😀
Recess	☹ 😐 🙂 😀
Birthday Parties	☹ 😐 🙂 😀
Sports	☹ 😐 🙂 😀
Robots	☹ 😐 🙂 😀

CARRYOVER ACTIVITY: DESCRIBING

Once you can say the R sound in speech therapy, it is important to work on carrying that skill over to connected speech/conversation. Even if you can say the R sound perfectly in sentences, it can be tricky to remember it when you are chatting with your friends. This activity will help you practice your R sound in connected speech.

Directions: Write six things you would like to describe in the spaces below. You will talk about the items/events. You will describe them in detail. Be sure to think about your R sound while you are talking. Once you're done, rate how you think you did by marking one of the faces.

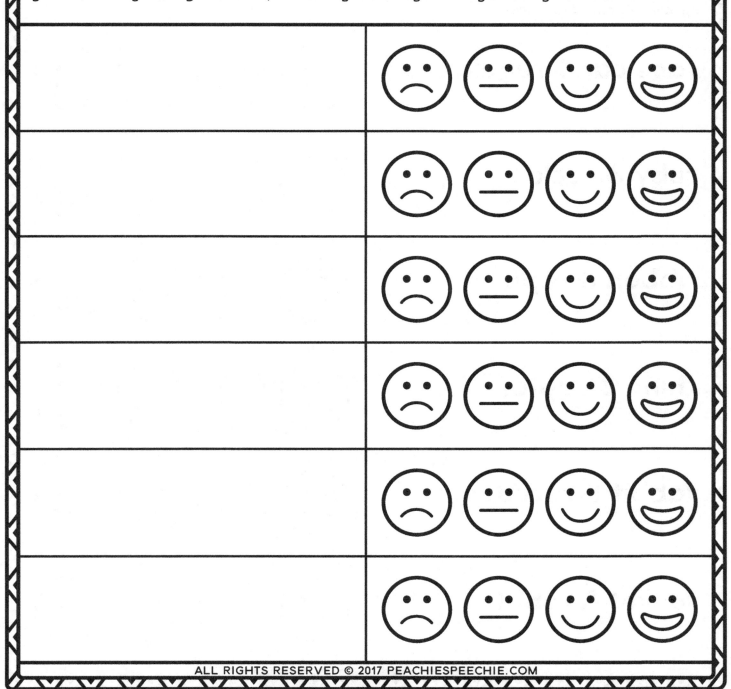

CARRYOVER ACTIVITY: COMPARE & CONTRAST

INITIAL R

Once you can say the R sound in speech therapy, it is important to work on carrying that skill over to connected speech/conversation. Even if you can say the R sound perfectly in sentences, it can be tricky to remember it when you are chatting with your friends. This activity will help you practice your R sound in connected speech.

Directions: You will talk about the items listed below. You will compare and contrast them. That means you will be telling how they are the same and how they are different. Be sure to think about your R sound while you are talking. Once you're done, rate how you think you did by marking one of the faces.

race car & regular car	☹ 😐 🙂 😃
ruby & rock	☹ 😐 🙂 😃
ribbon & rope	☹ 😐 🙂 😃
rhino & raptor	☹ 😐 🙂 😃
rabbit & raccoon	☹ 😐 🙂 😃
rocket & robot	☹ 😐 🙂 😃

CARRYOVER ACTIVITY: COMPARE & CONTRAST

VOCALIC R - MEDIAL AND FINAL

Once you can say the R sound in speech therapy, it is important to work on carrying that skill over to connected speech/conversation. Even if you can say the R sound perfectly in sentences, it can be tricky to remember it when you are chatting with your friends. This activity will help you practice your R sound in connected speech.

Directions: You will talk about the items listed below. You will compare and contrast them. That means you will be telling how they are the same and how they are different. Be sure to think about your R sound while you are talking. Once you're done, rate how you think you did by marking one of the faces.

bear & tiger	☹ 😐 🙂 😀
sweater & skirt	☹ 😐 🙂 😀
paper & marker	☹ 😐 🙂 😀
hammer & scissors	☹ 😐 🙂 😀
lizard & alligator	☹ 😐 🙂 😀
shirt & shorts	☹ 😐 🙂 😀

CARRYOVER ACTIVITY: COMPARE & CONTRAST

R BLENDS

Once you can say the R sound in speech therapy, it is important to work on carrying that skill over to connected speech/conversation. Even if you can say the R sound perfectly in sentences, it can be tricky to remember it when you are chatting with your friends. This activity will help you practice your R sound in connected speech.

Directions: You will talk about the items listed below. You will compare and contrast them. That means you will be telling how they are the same and how they are different. Be sure to think about your R sound while you are talking. Once you're done, rate how you think you did by marking one of the faces.

Tree & grass	☹ 😐 🙂 😄
Frog & dragon	☹ 😐 🙂 😄
Truck & tractor	☹ 😐 🙂 😄
Your friend & your grandpa	☹ 😐 🙂 😄
Prunes & grapes	☹ 😐 🙂 😄
Freeze pop & pretzel	☹ 😐 🙂 😄

CARRYOVER ACTIVITY: HOW-TO PRESENTATIONS

Once you can say the R sound in the speech room, it is important to work on carrying that skill over to connected speech/conversation. Even if you can say the R sound perfectly in sentences, it can be tricky to remember it when you are chatting with your friends. This activity will help you practice your R sound in connected speech.

Directions: You will be giving a mini presentation on how to do something. Take a moment to think about what you want to say. You can write notes about what words you want to use and what you want to say in the space provided. When you are ready, stand up and present. Be sure to think about your R sound while you're talking! Once you're done, rate how you think you did by marking one of the faces.

How to ride a bike	Notes:	How did I do? Needs improvement Good Awesome! Great R sounds!
How to play a sport (You decide which sport)	Notes:	How did I do? Needs improvement Good Awesome! Great R sounds!
How to say the R sound	Notes:	How did I do? Needs improvement Good Awesome! Great R sounds!
How to make a snack (You decide which snack)	Notes:	How did I do? Needs improvement Good Awesome! Great R sounds!

CARRYOVER ACTIVITY: HOW-TO PRESENTATIONS

Once you can say the R sound in the speech room, it is important to work on carrying that skill over to connected speech/conversation. Even if you can say the R sound perfectly in sentences, it can be tricky to remember it when you are chatting with your friends. This activity will help you practice your R sound in connected speech.

Directions: You will be giving a mini presentation on how to do something. Take a moment to think about what you want to say. You can write notes about what words you want to use and what you want to say in the space provided. When you are ready, stand up and present. Be sure to think about your R sound while you're talking! Once you're done, rate how you think you did by marking one of the faces.

How to study for a test	Notes:	How did I do? Needs improvement / Good / Awesome! Great R sounds!
How to convince your parents to let you do something	Notes:	How did I do? Needs improvement / Good / Awesome! Great R sounds!
How to make a new friend	Notes:	How did I do? Needs improvement / Good / Awesome! Great R sounds!
How to clean your room	Notes:	How did I do? Needs improvement / Good / Awesome! Great R sounds!

CARRYOVER ACTIVITY: HOW-TO PRESENTATIONS

Once you can say the R sound in the speech room, it is important to work on carrying that skill over to connected speech/conversation. Even if you can say the R sound perfectly in sentences, it can be tricky to remember it when you are chatting with your friends. This activity will help you practice your R sound in connected speech.

Directions: You will be giving a mini presentation on how to do something. Take a moment to think about what you want to say. You can write notes about what words you want to use and what you want to say in the space provided. When you are ready, stand up and present. Be sure to think about your R sound while you're talking! Once you're done, rate how you think you did by marking one of the faces.

How to deal with a bully	Notes:	How did I do? Needs improvement Good Awesome! Great R sounds!
How to prepare for a party	Notes:	How did I do? Needs improvement Good Awesome! Great R sounds!
How to make cookies	Notes:	How did I do? Needs improvement Good Awesome! Great R sounds!
How to build a sandcastle	Notes:	How did I do? Needs improvement Good Awesome! Great R sounds!

CARRYOVER ACTIVITY: HOW-TO PRESENTATIONS

Once you can say the R sound in the speech room, it is important to work on carrying that skill over to connected speech/conversation. Even if you can say the R sound perfectly in sentences, it can be tricky to remember it when you are chatting with your friends. This activity will help you practice your R sound in connected speech.

Directions: You will be giving a mini presentation on how to do something. Take a moment to think about what you want to say. You can write notes about what words you want to use and what you want to say in the space provided. When you are ready, stand up and present. Be sure to think about your R sound while you're talking! Once you're done, rate how you think you did by marking one of the faces.

Write your presentation topic.	Notes:	How did I do?
		Needs improvement
		Good
		Awesome! Great R sounds!
Write your presentation topic.	Notes:	How did I do?
		Needs improvement
		Good
		Awesome! Great R sounds!
Write your presentation topic.	Notes:	How did I do?
		Needs improvement
		Good
		Awesome! Great R sounds!
Write your presentation topic.	Notes:	How did I do?
		Needs improvement
		Good
		Awesome! Great R sounds!

CARRYOVER ACTIVITY: TELL A STORY

To practice your R sound in connected speech, you are going to tell a story. First, you will map out your story below. Give your characters names that have the R sound in them and try to use lots of R words throughout the story. After you've completed the story map, you will write and illustrate your story on the next page.

Characters

Setting

Beginning

Middle

End

Additional notes

CARRYOVER ACTIVITY: TELL A STORY

Use your story map on the previous page to help you write your story. You can also illustrate your story in the space provided. Then, tell your story to your SLP, helper, or friend.

_____

_____

_____

_____

_____

_____

_____

_____

Illustrate your story

RESOURCES

Bauman-Wangler, J. (2008). *Articulatory and phonological impairments: A clinical focus.* (3rd ed.) Boston, MA: Pearson Education, Inc.

Berthnal, J., Bankston, N., Flipsen P. (2009). *Articulation and Phonological Disorders: Speech Sound Disorders in Children.* (6th ed.) Boston, MA: Pearson Education, Inc.

Cummings, A., Hallgrimson, J., & Robinson, S. (2019) *Speech Intervention Outcomes Associated with Word Lexicality and Intervention Intensity.* Language, Speech, and Hearing Services in Schools, 50, 83-98

Fry, E. (1997). 1000 Instant Words: *The Most Common Words for Teaching Reading, Writing, and Spelling.* Chicago, IL: Contemporary Books

Henderson Jones, P. (2004) *Eureka! Finding the Elusive Vocalic R Sounds.* Advance for Speech-Language Pathologists & Audiologists, 14(21), 19.

Marshalla, P. (2011). *Successful R Therapy.* Mill Creek, WA: Marshalla Speech and Language.

Rusiewicz, H., & Rivera, J. (2017) *The Effect of Hand Gesture Cues Within the Treatment of /r/ for a College-Aged Adult with Persisting Childhood Apraxia of Speech.* American Journal of Speech-Language Pathology, 26, 1236-1243.

Secord, W (2007). *Eliciting Sounds: Techniques for Clinicians.* (2nd ed.) Clifton Park, NY: Thomson Delmar Learning.

Watt, J. (2006). *Speech Therapy Paired Stimulation for R Sound.* Pennridge School District http://www.speakingofspeech.info/ArticR/R-PairedstimulationKARLA.pdf